# Emotionally HAPPY HOMES®

Transform, understand and manage your emotional stress

Jules O'Neill

Emotionally Happy Homes® : Transform, understand and manage your emotional stress

Author – Jules O'Neill

© Jules O'Neill 2019

www.julesoneill.com
info@julesoneill.com

The material in this publication is of the nature of general comment only and does not represent any professional advice. The author of this book does not dispense medical advice or prescribe the use of any technique as a form of treatment for physical, emotional or medical problems without the advice of a physician, either directly or indirectly.

The intent of the author is only to offer information of a general nature to help you in your quest for emotional and spiritual wellbeing. It is not intended to provide specific guidance for particular circumstances, and it should not be relied on as the basis for any decision to take action or not take action on any matter which it covers.

Readers should obtain professional advice where appropriate, before making any such decision. To the maximum extent permitted by law, the author disclaims all responsibility and liability to any person, arising directly or indirectly from any person taking or not taking action based on the information in this publication.

All rights reserved. Except as permitted under the Australian Copyright Act 1968 (for example, a fair dealing for the purposes of study, research, criticism or review), no part of this book may be reproduced by any mechanical, photographic or electronic process or in the form of a phonographic recording; nor may it be stored in a retrieval system, transmitted or otherwise copied for public or private use – other than for 'fair use' as brief quotations embodied in articles and reviews – without prior written permission of the publisher. All enquiries should be made at the address above.

Editing, design and publishing support by www.AuthorSupportServices.com

ISBN: 978-0-9923215-0-5

A catalogue record for this book is available from the National Library of Australia

I dedicate this book to my three children.

Thank you for being my biggest teachers and for gifting me with endless warm moments, fond memories, funny times, joy, growth and evolution. I am so grateful you're in my life.

# What People Are Saying...

"Empowered is the first feeling that comes to me. Learning tools to help me consciously live my today to create an amazing tomorrow! I love that!" PC – Sunshine Coast, QLD

"Learning how other people's stuff in the home can affect us and understanding how to stop this is incredible." TB – Brisbane, QLD

"My family life and all my relationships have really benefited and are so much more harmonious." SW – Glass House Mountains, QLD

"After reading this book, I can now see what's really going on with my teenagers. Our relationship has changed so much for the better as a result." GH – Bondi, NSW

"It's been so useful and helped us as a family to understand what's really going on between each other in the home environment. We are becoming closer and more connected each day." IL – Baulkham Hills, NSW

"My emotions are now something I look forward to feeling and exploring, rather than blaming others for and reaching for alcohol to dull. I see my emotions as a messenger from my angels. As a result, I have now opened up my creative channels and started a small business. My home and family are my biggest supporters, whereas once I felt they all held me back. All that changed was ME! I changed on the inside, and my outside reflects this." JM – New Farm, QLD

"These methods take you to what's really going on. That clarity allows me to support myself and my children in the best way. I've stopped being reactive to the emotions of others. It also helps me to hold the space with my husband, allowing us to reach common ground and both grow." BD – Geneva, Switzerland

"This book has presented me with tools to grow that I have not found elsewhere. I now have a great balance between work and family, and even make time for my own development. I write specifically for the guys out there that have found themselves in a place not where they truly wish to be. Emotional intelligence, consciousness and self-awareness are not the yarns you'll have at the pub with the boys. It's been a gap in this macho world of ours. It's not anymore." BA – Perth, WA

"I am so grateful to the tools in this book for all the wonderful results that I see with my daughter! It is like a load has been lifted from my mind or a flower blooming in spring to watch her just be the most amazing girl that she is! My darling girl has had some great frustrations and has found it very difficult to express herself, both at school and home. She is communicating to us now that she is aware of how she behaves and how she appears to others. She understands that when you are nice to others, they are nice back!" AK – Auckland, New Zealand

# Acknowledgements

I would love to give oceans of gratitude to my clients. Thank you for trusting me, believing in me and encouraging me to share the wisdom that is continually co-created and comes through each and every session.

Oceans of gratitude also to all my students who have attended Body Consciousness® and Women's Wisdom® workshops and classes.

More oceans of gratitude to the many awesome and amazing mentors, both human and celestial, whom I've received so much from throughout my life so far.

Yet more oceans of gratitude, especially to my family and friends. Neither I nor this book would be here without your continued support, love and encouragement.

Finally, oceans of gratitude to YOU, the reader reading this right now. I value, honour, appreciate and respect your quest to continually show up as the best version of yourself and share more of who you are. I also honour your desire for both your family and yourself to be in a place of emotional peace, via your heart and inner wisdom.

Never, never, never give up on living the life you imagined. It is here, eternally, for us all!

# Foreword

## by Nicole Collins

I remember now with clarity the joy, delight, synchronicity, focus, play, drive and 'anything is possible' of my teens up to my late 20s. Life was exciting, and there was nothing and no one that would hold me back. Show me an opportunity and I would be two feet in. Perhaps on occasion to my detriment, the 'fools rush in' saying comes to mind. However, even when I did rush in and potentially made a mess, I always had the self-confidence that I could undo it and move on.

Somewhere around the time of having children and stopping paid work, however, I began to disconnect from me. With the benefit of hindsight, I believe I disconnected from my personal beliefs and started connecting with the beliefs of mass consciousness. These are the beliefs that we always see in the media, where there is drama, blame, manipulation, division and hurt, where you need to struggle to make something work, and so on. I can look back now and clearly see how I withdrew from my personal beliefs and dimmed the clarity, joy, delight, ambition, focus, play, drive and sense that 'anything is possible'.

I am not saying for an instant that I was not happy or grateful. I was. However, with the benefit of hindsight, I can see that in adopting these new mass consciousness beliefs, I began to blame others when I wasn't happy, rather than looking within myself for the real cause.

For all intents and purposes, everything seemed perfect. I had a hard-working, loving, supportive partner; lived in a lovely home; had three beautiful children to care for; and had many friends.

So why was there discontent?

Like many do in life, I just pushed things aside and 'got on with it'. I did not realise at the time, but what I was actually doing was suppressing and internalising. I accumulated stories and beliefs that "I won't be received if I ask for what I want," and "I can't do something for me, because I have to support my partner."

I found that with this suppression came blame, and that's what I ended up verbalising instead of my desires and dreams. These accumulated stories and beliefs effectively wrote new patterns and programs of who I saw myself as.

I realised around the time my children were ten that I had internalised so much and had dug a hole of blame so deep that I would struggle to articulate my dreams or desires. In fact, I couldn't even see them. My focus was that of a scattergun, trying to touch as many things as possible.

I would stand on the sidelines of my life, watching and waiting for something to go wrong so I could jump in and fix it. What a mixed-up creation I was living, sitting there waiting and almost wishing for something to go wrong so I could 'help'. I had so diluted the essence of who I was in my teens and 20s that I was no longer recognisable, even to myself.

Something had to change.

It was around this time that I reconnected with Jules O'Neill. Jules and I had known each other since our children were in kindergarten. However, our lives had taken us on different paths for a time.

We both lived on the Sunshine Coast, north of Brisbane, and our reconnection started with VERY early morning beach walks. During these walks, Jules introduced me to self-muscle testing and energetic awareness of what really is going on in our bodies. Here began my journey of becoming a master untier of emotional knots, which opened a new world of unlimited possibilities.

This was no quick fix. We all carry ancestral patterns and programs, as well as programs we have taken on ourselves, either consciously or unconsciously. However, over time, I became a more confident, empowered individual. My focus and creativity returned with more clarity than I had ever had. I started to bravely share my wisdom and dreams at home.

To my delight, that bravery was received with enthusiasm from my husband, Shane. The stories and irrational beliefs that I had held so dear for so long ended up being seen as just that: stories and irrational beliefs.

Of course, I had a partner who wanted to see me thrive and do what I love, and that is how I was received. Well, for the most part. I have still had to learn how to express myself authentically from my heart. That takes some practice, but when I don't get it exactly right, I know now that all I need to do is 'lean in' to that space with care and awareness, and unravel that little knot.

I have worked together with Jules for eight years now. It has been a phenomenal time of growth, fun, challenges, learning and awareness. I have learnt that I can best contribute to my family and friends by getting out of my past stories of lack and blame, and sharing the wisdom of tools we jointly refined over our friendship.

The shift in my relationships has been nothing short of life-changing.

This is not the finish line. I believe it is just the start. But I stand on this start line with an excited body, looking forward. I do this because I have seen the change so far and so have my family and friends.

There are still challenges. That is one of the things we are assured of in life. However, I now have the tools to lean in to those challenges with curiosity and awareness, knowing I can move through them with lightness. I live in an emotionally happy home, which I love and am grateful for. Life is an exciting adventure filled with joy once more.

I challenge you to value yourself enough to 'lean in' to your life with curiosity and believe it is possible for YOU to live in an emotionally happy home too.

YOU are worth it.

"Life can offer up the strangest of events and circumstances with the intent to only always open your heart and break down judgements in your mind.

You have a choice in how you occur through them. Stay light and find your place of laughter. Ride the eagle on wings of grace, holding your head high and opening your smile wide and warm.

Let go of any choice where you are carried by the eagle's claws as a victim proclaiming you can do nothing about your direction.

Both choices will take you to heights beyond what you imagine. It is up to you how you like to travel."

– Jules O'Neill

# Contents

| | | |
|---|---|---:|
| Introduction | | 1 |
| Chapter 1: | What IS an Emotionally Happy Home? | 11 |
| Chapter 2: | Emotionally Happy Homes Basics | 31 |
| Chapter 3: | Understanding Emotions in Depth | 51 |
| Chapter 4: | Understanding Emotional Stress | 67 |
| Chapter 5: | How to Manage Emotional Stress | 91 |
| Chapter 6: | Personal Emotional Hygiene | 119 |
| Chapter 7: | Emotional Hygiene for Other People's Emotional Stress | 139 |
| Conclusion | | 173 |
| Need a Little More Support? | | 179 |
| About the Author | | 181 |
| Appendix A: Negative Emotions | | 183 |
| Appendix B: Positive Emotions | | 195 |
| Appendix C: Reactive Behaviours | | 207 |

# Introduction

## Do you wish something in your life were different?

If you're like most people I've met and worked with, your life is a mixed bag of 'good' and 'bad' stuff.

You have a family you love at some level, whether that's your childhood family or the one you live with now… although sometimes they really drive you crazy.

You have a job that pays your bills… although it doesn't fill you with excitement when you wake up on a Monday morning.

And you've done a bit of reading on how to be a better, happier human being… although figuring out how to put it all into practice is SO much harder than it seems on the surface.

In other words, you know you're not doing too badly, all things considered. You know other people have it far worse.

But, at the same time, you really, really wish something – perhaps *more* than one 'somethings' – were different in your life

## If so, I get it

I've worked with tens of thousands of people over two decades, and most of them started in the same place you're at now. In fact, some of them started convinced that nothing was right in their lives – and that nothing could ever be right again.

Here's just a sample of the types of comments I've heard from people at the point they first started working with me or attending my workshops:

> "I want to be a friendly, loving and supportive partner. I want a marriage that energises and inspires me, where we both laugh often and look forward to lovemaking. Instead, I find myself constantly snapping at my partner. The closest we've come to a romantic conversation lately is figuring out who's picking up our child from school or which bill to pay first."

> "I want to spend quality time with my kids in a home that feels peaceful, relaxed and loving. I long for them to see me as a positive role model. Instead, they're glued to the TV or their devices. I feel like I'm always either yelling or biting my tongue – and if I get one more eye-roll or sarcastic comment from my teen, I swear I'm going to lose it."

> "I want to feel like I'm doing something that matters with my life – and getting paid well for it. I want to feel excited about my work in the world – knowing exactly how it makes a difference and that it's using my unique skills. I also want a richly abundant life OUTSIDE of my work. Instead, I'm caught in a nine-to-five grind with work that crushes my soul, barely helps me make ends meet and creates no real value for the planet."

> "I want to feel good within my body – vital, energised and full of life. I want to eat food that nourishes me, move in a way that feels good and get restful, relaxing sleep again. I want to do all the things I know I *should* do to look after myself. Instead, I constantly work late, live off caffeine and convenience food, and I'm lucky if I get six hours sleep a night. I don't even recognise the person I see in the mirror any more."

## Maybe you see yourself in one of those comments?

In fact, maybe you see yourself in more than one of them.

If so, I have good news: life doesn't have to stay that way. You *can* have the experiences you want. You can have the relationships you want, the career you want and the health you want.

You can have ANYTHING, in fact, that your heart desires.

And the news gets better. Not only can you have what you want but you already have everything you need inside you to help you figure out how to get it. You have access to the guidance and support of the entire universe within your heart and higher self.

Even better yet: if you get still and commit to truly listening to your heart, it will tell you what you need to do next. It will guide you along the path you need to walk.

The only catch is that the language it speaks to help you become aware of this path isn't one of words. Instead, it's one of emotions and feelings.

But… creating anything your heart desires is simple and effortless when you understand your emotions and what they're saying.

> Creating anything your heart desires is simple and effortless when you understand your emotions and what they're saying.

I know for a fact this is true because I've seen it play out over and over and over again in the lives, relationships and careers of my clients and workshop participants. I've seen people go on to:

- build seven-figure businesses
- heal chronic physical illnesses
- heal apparently irreparable relationships
- create amazing, harmonious homes
- live happy, peaceful, simple lives, full of warmth, creativity and connection.

And it all started with learning to listen to what their emotions were telling them.

## This book is about more than just 'managing emotions'

On the surface, this book is about learning to work with your emotions. And, as you read it, you'll learn a LOT about them.

You'll learn what emotions are, how they differ from feelings and how to hear the messages they have for you. You'll learn about emotional stress, which lies beneath so many of the physical, mental and spiritual ills we suffer from as individuals and on a societal level. And you'll learn about emotional hygiene – the practices and routines you can use to keep yourself emotionally clean and healthy.

> There's so much more to working with emotions than how you feel in the moment.

It's true that learning to work with your emotions in this way feels good internally. And that's important for reasons you'll learn about later in the book.

But the results don't stop inside you. There's so much more to working with emotions than how you feel in the moment. As my clients and workshop participants have discovered, this kind of work also helps them to create the relationships, homes, careers, health and lives that they want.

The book you're holding in your hands lays out exactly how to create all of these things. In it, you'll learn:

- how to hear and become aware of what your emotions are telling you
- how to value what you learn and act on that wisdom, instead of discounting it and doubting yourself
- how to stop reacting to unwanted situations and instead respond in ways that actively *create* your ideal situations
- how to keep yourself from taking your emotional stress out on other people
- how to recognise (and dismantle) patterns and programs you've inherited from your childhood family that block you from creating what you want in life
- how to choose the emotion you feel if you don't like the one you're experiencing in the moment
- how to express your authentic self with love, kindness and courage, regardless of the challenging situations you find yourself in
- how to experience peace, harmony and flow in all areas of your life.

## Everything starts at home

If emotions play such a major role in creating ALL aspects of our lives, you might wonder why I focus this book on 'emotionally happy homes'. Why don't I talk about having an 'emotionally happy career' or an 'emotionally happy body' instead?

The answer is a concept you'll meet in Chapter 1, which is that 'who you are at home is who you are'. You're never more authentically 'you' than you are when you're at home. All the masks come off. All the facades you fight to hold up while you're out in the world come crumbling down the moment you walk through your front door.

That means if you can figure out this 'emotional happiness stuff' at home, you can literally figure it out anywhere. If you can manage your emotional stress at home, managing it in your workplace becomes a breeze. And if you can practise emotional hygiene at home, you can meet every situation in the rest of your life with the calmness, compassion and optimism that comes from being emotionally healthy.

## There's a difference between simple and easy

As you work your way through this book, I want you to keep in mind that although the techniques you'll learn are simple, they're not always easy.

> If you use the tools in this book, you don't need to get it right first time, every time for your life to improve immeasurably.

They take practice – sometimes a LOT of practice – before they become second nature. In the meantime, they can feel like a struggle. Sometimes you'll drop the ball and get it horribly, horribly wrong. Even once you've been doing this work for a while, your emotional reactions can still take you by surprise sometimes.

But that's OK: if you use the tools in this book, you don't need to get it right first time, every time for your life to improve immeasurably. You're allowed to make mistakes, so be gentle with yourself.

On top of that, some of the concepts you'll come across can be immensely confronting the first time you meet them. In fact, some of them can be confronting for quite some time afterwards too.

Here's an example of when that happened with a long-term client who'd also taken several of my workshops.

> ## Sarah's story: being willing to check in
>
> As I was working on this book with my awesome editor, I showed the first chapter to a long-term client, Sarah (not her real name). Now, Sarah had worked with me for over 16 years so she wasn't a newcomer to personal development. She'd been exploring and defusing her 'stuff' for over a decade.
>
> Still, though, when she read the first few pages of the first chapter, Sarah noticed a wobble. (You'll learn more about this term in Chapter 2.) She noticed that she was actively *looking* for something to criticise in the book.
>
> With a sense of open curiosity, both of us checked in with our feeling bodies. (You'll learn more about checking in throughout the book, but especially in Chapter 6.)
>
> I felt peaceful about everything in the book. Sarah, however, discovered she had something going on beneath the surface.
>
> Soon after she started exploring what that might be, she texted me to say that she'd somehow broken her chest of drawers. Apparently, one of the drawers was completely stuck and wouldn't move. Most people would assume this was coincidental, but Sarah knew better. (You'll find out why in Chapter 5.)
>
> As she compassionately and non-judgementally allowed her knowing to surface, she uncovered a hidden belief that she 'didn't DESERVE an emotionally happy home'.
>
> Then, as she explored this programming, she realised she'd grown up believing that expecting this kind of happiness for herself was selfish.

> So coming across a guide that promised to help her create that happiness generated a level of inner conflict.
>
> As soon as she identified and rewrote her belief, the trigger disappeared. Soon afterwards, she wrote back to me saying, "I finished reading the chapter. I LOVE it: it challenges me, but I got SO MUCH out of reading it ♥ ♥ ♥."

Imagine, though, that Sarah hadn't been willing to explore what was going on for her. Imagine if she'd instead said, "Look, I've been working on this stuff for 16 years with you. I'm an expert at it now, so I think I'd know if I were just being triggered. This is NOT about my beliefs or patterns!"

If she'd reacted that way, she'd have missed out on the gold she soon discovered in that first chapter. That doesn't even begin to consider what she might later get out of the rest of the book.

Plus, because she's a human being – just like all of us – my choice to not immediately agree that she was 'right' about the book content might have triggered her further. And if she hadn't been willing to take responsibility for and resolve THAT, who knows how it might have affected our relationship in the future?

Luckily, she *was* willing to explore and check in. But many of us aren't. Instead, we double down and accept our reactions at their surface value.

Because, let's face it, this stuff ISN'T comfortable or easy.

## I want to encourage you to do the same thing Sarah did

As you're reading through this book, you may well experience the same kind of wobbly reaction that Sarah did. It might be due to a completely different hidden belief… or you may have echoes of the same one she did.

Regardless, you may find yourself feeling angry, frustrated or annoyed by particular chapters or sections, or even just specific concepts.

If so, I'm going to encourage you to do exactly what she did: check in with your emotions. Use the techniques you'll learn as you read through these pages to ask your heart and higher self what's REALLY going on. Then listen for the answers.

I promise you… they'll come.

## You CAN choose to live in an emotionally happy home

Again, I want to come back to my earlier promise to you. You CAN have an emotionally happy home – and, because of it, an emotionally happy life.

> You CAN have an emotionally happy home – and, because of it, an emotionally happy life.

The first step is to block out some time when you won't be disturbed, grab a pen, highlighter and paper, and sit down somewhere comfortable. Then, as you explore the pages of this book, do your best to stay open-minded. Notice if anything creates a reaction within you – and if it does, do your best to lean in to that reaction.

I also recommend using your highlighter to mark any quotes, passages or paragraphs that really resonate for you as you read. Bookmark key concepts so you can come back to them over and over again.

At the end of each chapter, you'll find exercises that will help reinforce the information you've learnt. Then, at the end of the book, you'll find a set of appendices that you can photocopy and place somewhere you'll see them regularly.

This book contains ALL the tools you need to start creating your emotionally happy home.

I hope you enjoy using them!

OCEANS OF LOVE

*Jules xx*

CHAPTER 1

# What IS an Emotionally Happy Home?

*For many years, I've been teaching people how to be emotionally happy within themselves, their homes and their families. In this chapter, I'll introduce you to what an emotionally happy home is, and why life is so much better when you live in one.*

## What IS an 'emotionally happy home'?

Throughout this book, I'm going to talk about how to create and maintain an 'emotionally happy home'. When I use this term, I'm talking about a culture in which everyone in the home pays attention to – and takes responsibility for – their own emotions.

It's a culture in which everyone manages their own emotional stress and practises their own emotional hygiene to explore what's really going on for them. (You'll learn a little about both these concepts later in this chapter.) Then, when these practices help them to uncover essential insights, each person feels safe sharing those insights with the people they care about.

An emotionally happy home culture is also one in which each person uses their emotional insights to make real changes in their life. They take action to finetune what's working and fix what isn't – both inside their home and outside of it.

And, finally, it's a culture in which everyone supports and celebrates each other's growth. A culture in which everyone's motivated by what they can contribute to each other, rather than what they want or need to 'get'.

Does that sound like the kind of culture you'd love in your home?

It's certainly the culture I love in mine!

## ANYONE can live in an emotionally happy home

Before I say anything else, I want to make something clear. *Anyone* can have an emotionally happy home, regardless of their family configuration. That means that you – and your home – can be emotionally happy, regardless of your age, gender or sexual orientation, or whether:

- you live in a 'traditional' family with a partner/spouse and children
- you're a single parent who's raising your kids on your own
- you live with a partner or spouse without children
- you live in shared accommodation with flatmates
- you live completely on your own.

We'll talk more in later chapters about how to manage emotional stress and practise emotional hygiene when you don't have a partner or kids. For the moment, just understand that the home you are living in right now CAN be an emotionally happy one.

You simply need to learn (and then put some effort into practising) a few core skills first.

*Note: Before we continue, let's get on the same page about the definitions of the different 'family' terms I refer to throughout this book.*

*When I use the term 'childhood family', I am referring to the family you grew up with: your parents, siblings, step-parents, step-siblings, adoptive parents, all extended family members and caretakers.*

*When I use the term 'family', I am referring to your present family today. These are the people you've chosen and created as your family and choose to connect with as an adult: your partner, children, grandchildren, in-laws and any childhood family members you are still in contact with today.*

## The benefits of living in an emotionally happy home

So why would you *want* to live in an emotionally happy home? In a general sense, being emotionally happy at home is important because who you are at home is your dominant vibration to the universe.

> Who you are at home is your dominant vibration to the universe.

You're the most real 'you' possible when you're at home with your family or flatmates. You take off all the masks you wear at work or when you're out with friends, and become the person you really are. So whatever you focus on and experience at home when you're being that 'you' is what you send out to the universe and create more of.

In other words, if you want a life that feels emotionally peaceful, calm, caring and joyful, you need to create a home that feels that way.

If you're looking for more specific reasons to maintain an emotionally happy home, here are just a few of the top ones:

- **First and foremost, it's about safety.** An emotionally happy home is a place you truly enjoy being. It's a safe, warm, loving environment in which you can grow and develop into the best version of yourself.

- **Second, it's about contribution.** When you create an emotionally happy home, you support everyone else who lives there in feeling safe, warm and loved, and becoming the best versions of themselves too.

- **Third, it's about growing braver.** It takes real courage to live out the principles and practices of an emotionally happy home. That courage will expand out into other areas of your life, giving you a resource to draw on in situations outside of your home as well.

- **Fourth, it's about you and what's in your heart.** It's about using your emotions to discover whatever's in there for you. Then, when you live via your heart, you'll love who you are and know what you're here to do. And when you do *this*, you'll naturally feel as though you're enough.

- **Fifth, it's about becoming more creative.** When you're no longer constantly stuck in emotional stress, you'll discover creative dreams and callings you had no idea existed. You'll find yourself drawn to creative activities that give you a sense of pleasure and satisfaction you didn't realise were missing.

- **Sixth, it's about getting healthier.** Living in constant emotional stress takes an immense toll on both your physical and mental health. Learning to manage that stress can reduce your chances of developing physical and mental illnesses. It can also help you to make better, healthier choices in your everyday life.

🎗 **Finally, it's about experiencing real abundance.** You'll discover the true meaning of abundance. This doesn't necessarily mean that millions of dollars will suddenly appear. Rather, you'll start to experience a constant flow of gifts and peaceful feelings in your life.

*"When you tend to the Emotional Journey this universe has the resources and the cleverness to orchestrate for each of you exactly what you want..."*

– Abraham Hicks

## Living in an emotionally happy home means honouring emotions

In an emotionally happy home, you – along with everyone else – recognise that emotions are important. You recognise that your emotions provide crystal clear internal guidance about what's going on below the surface for you.

You also recognise that your emotions pinpoint unconscious beliefs that are at odds with what your heart and higher self are saying. Your emotions are always – *only always* – also an

> In an emotionally happy home, you – along with everyone else – recognise that emotions are important.

alarm bell that sounds an unmistakable warning when you're moving in a direction or thinking thoughts that are not in alignment with your heart and higher self.

*Note: throughout this book, you'll hear the phrase 'only always' a LOT. When I use it, I'm taking a step up from just saying 'always'. 'Only always' means absolutely no exceptions or exclusions. It's an order of magnitude more 'always' than 'always'.*

Because you recognise these things, you honour both your own emotions and those of everyone else in your home. You know that even if an emotion is intense or extremely uncomfortable, it will pass. You also know that if you honour an emotion, you'll get to receive the gifts of wisdom it offers.

For example, if you pay attention to an intense emotion and work with it, you might find it offers you guidance on:

- which foods or activities are most healthy for you
- which actions will create the most energy and vitality for you
- how best to express your creativity
- what things are best for you to spend your money on
- how hard you work and how much time you spend at your job.

… and so much more.

Paying attention to your emotions about these things will help you to make the best possible choices for you. Creating a culture where everyone else in your home feels safe paying attention to and honouring their own feelings will help them to do the same thing.

## It also means taking RESPONSIBILITY for your emotions

Often, when you're in the middle of a 'wobble' – an unpleasant emotional reaction – it's easy to blame other people. You tell yourself that the way you feel is 'their fault' and that if they just changed their behaviour to meet your expectations, everything would be fine.

The truth is that your emotions are *your* responsibility to manage. The fact that you're feeling a strong emotion is a clear flashing sign that something inside you needs attention. Once you start to explore the emotion, you might discover that this 'something' is:

> The truth is that your emotions are *your* responsibility to manage.

- tolerating a behaviour you don't enjoy because you're uncomfortable talking about it with the person concerned
- giving your time, energy or money to something that feels inauthentic and out of alignment with the direction your heart and higher self are nudging you in
- not taking responsibility for something that happened in your past, which is now repeating itself in the present
- being stuck in an unconscious pattern based on limiting beliefs you've yet to discover.

Uncovering any of these things at play is wonderful, because only once you uncover the truth about what needs attention can you change it.

And that, in turn, is great news, because it means that your emotional happiness is something you can create and cultivate yourself.

## An emotionally happy home makes everyone feel safe

It's impossible to overstate just how important feeling safe is in creating an emotionally happy home. You can't honour and prioritise your emotions unless you feel safe doing so.

In practice, 'feeling safe' means creating a three-part agreement in your home about emotions. Ideally, everyone in your house will be part of this agreement, but it's totally OK if you just start by making the agreement with yourself. Your partner, kids or flatmates can always join you later in your journey when they're ready to.

- The first part of the agreement involves agreeing that experiencing emotions is more than just accepted. *It's expected.* It's something that all of you will do at some point. And it's not something that anyone should make themselves or anyone else feel wrong about.

- The second part is agreeing that everyone is responsible for their own emotions. Just knowing that you're not responsible for how anyone else feels – and that nobody is responsible for how you feel – is a huge step towards creating safety.

- The third part is agreeing that you have a choice about your emotions. Once you've developed the skills of emotional stress management and emotional hygiene, you're not stuck feeling uncomfortable, unpleasant emotions forever. It's possible to actively transform them if you want to.

This three-part agreement is really what I mean when I talk about the concept of 'emotional maturity' later in the book. For now, though, just know that when you agree to these three things, it suddenly becomes safe to acknowledge, explore and transform your emotions.

Only when *that* happens will your emotions finally reveal their gifts for you.

## The two core skills for an emotionally happy home

Once you've made your home a safe space in which to experience, explore and be guided by your emotions, there are two core skills you need to master. These skills are 'managing emotional stress' and 'practising emotional hygiene'; together, they create the practices that will lead to an emotionally happy home.

Here's a quick overview of what I mean by each term.

> Together, managing emotional stress and practising emotional hygiene create the practices that lead to an emotionally happy home.

- **Managing emotional stress**: this is something you do reactively when you've noticed you're beginning to emotionally wobble. It's like applying first aid to stop the bleeding when you've cut yourself. Emotional stress management ensures you don't make the injury worse, stops it from getting infected and helps it to heal as quickly as possible.

    However, you'll never be without *some* emotional stress in your life, and you'll learn more about how exactly to manage it in Chapters 4 and 5.

- **Practising emotional hygiene**: this is something you proactively do every day to help you avoid unnecessary emotional wobbles. It's like taking smart precautions to avoid cutting yourself in the first place, such as learning knife skills, keeping your knife sharp and drying your hands thoroughly before picking it up.

    Another way to see emotional hygiene is as being very similar to physical hygiene. You use emotional hygiene techniques just the same way that you wash your hands, shower and put on clean clothes to avoid smelling bad and spreading infection.

You'll learn more about how to practise emotional hygiene in Chapters 6 and 7.

## You won't get it 100% right all the time

Think back to the first time you rode a bicycle as a child. Unless you're very unusual, you didn't do a perfect job on the very first go.

You probably felt wobbly and uncoordinated. Maybe staying balanced required you to use muscles you didn't know you had before. You might even have fallen off a few times and scraped your elbows or knees.

Eventually, though, if you were willing to repeatedly put in time and practice, you got pretty good at it. And, finally, it became second nature – another skill you'd mastered.

The skills you need to create and maintain an emotionally happy home are just the same. They'll feel awkward and unnatural to start with. You'll need to put time and effort into mastering them. But once you've done so, they'll become second nature.

Of course, there are still some situations where riding a bike can be hard, even after you've mastered the basics. If the ground is particularly rough and uneven, or you're cycling up an extremely steep hill, you'll probably struggle.

> No matter how good you are at managing emotional stress and practising emotional hygiene, you're going to 'fall off' some days.

You may even need to get off and walk for a bit.

And in the same way, no matter how good you are at managing emotional stress and practising emotional hygiene, you're going to 'fall off' some days. That's exactly what happened to me one weekend midway through writing this book...

## My story: Jules vs. the light switch – Part 1

One Saturday evening, I was reminded that even when you've been living the emotionally happy home culture for many years, there are still things left to learn.

I was getting ready for bed after an amazing evening with my two teenaged children and their partners. There'd been five of us gathered around the dinner table that night. We'd eaten delicious food, shared the great things that had happened to each of us that day, and generally basked in the love and togetherness of the moment.

Then, around 8.30pm, as usual for me, I started to get ready for bed. My kids know that I get up at 4am most days, which means I choose to go to sleep early. They also know that if they switch any lights on, it's likely to wake me up. Our bulbs are bright and several of them shine straight into my bedroom.

On this evening, though, they both forgot.

First, ten minutes after I'd closed my eyes, my daughter went out into the kitchen with her partner to get a snack. She turned on the light as they chatted away, which wrenched me out of the sleep I'd almost settled into. And then, even worse, she LEFT it on when they retreated back to her bedroom.

I could feel myself starting to react at this point. My annoyance at what felt like *their* lack of consideration began to build.

Then, less than 20 minutes later, my son and his partner went out onto the verandah to enjoy the night air and chat. They also turned on all the lights and, once *again*, the bulbs shone straight into my room. And again, when they went back inside, they left the lights on.

My stress and irritation were really peaking now. I lay there fuming at *their* selfishness, and before I knew it, I'd jumped out of bed, determined to do something about it!

I strode to the closed door of my daughter's room, noticing that her light was off and that she and her partner were still talking quietly.

> Then without thinking about it, I opened her door, snaked my hand around, turned on her light switch and firmly shut the door again.
>
> The talking stopped abruptly, and I went back to my room, feeling as though I'd made my point.
>
> Of course, when I woke up the next morning, though, I felt much less happy with myself. I knew I'd reacted poorly from my stress and irritation. And I knew that meant I had some work to do to discover what was really going on inside me and then clean up the mess I'd made.
>
> Luckily, I had the tools on hand to help with that!

## Most homes today aren't emotionally happy

The 'reactive behaviour' I displayed in the story above is very unusual in my home. That's because all three of us who live there – both children and me – understand and practise the principles of an emotionally happy home culture.

However, in all too many homes today, reactive behaviours are the norm rather than the exception. And that in turn leads to a home in which:

- you or the people you live with experience constant emotional struggles and outbursts
- you regularly fight with members of your family or even with yourself
- you feel like you need to escape into addictions like drugs, alcohol, food, TV, work or anything else that 'numbs the pain'
- you feel separate, lonely and disconnected from the people around you
- you struggle to find enough time, money, ideas and love

🌿 you hate being at home and stay away as much as possible – perhaps making excuses like 'I have a busy life, and I need to earn money'.

That may be your reality as you're reading this book, but I promise you that it doesn't have to be that way. You can always – *only always* – change it.

## Understanding the difference between feelings and emotions

One principle that's fundamental to living in an emotionally happy home is that feelings and emotions are NOT the same things. They're both important to tune into and honour, but they communicate very different information.

🌿 **A feeling is an internal sensation that naturally finds you.** It's undeniable, and you can't argue with it or reason with it, so you have no choice about feeling it. It will continue until you take some kind of action to soothe it, and its purpose is to nourish, nurture or sustain your body. See the table below for a few examples of feelings.

🌿 **An emotion is the way you interpret or describe a feeling.** It's based on your thoughts and beliefs about the feeling you're experiencing. If you change your focus or thoughts about the feeling, you change your emotion. See the table on the next page for a few examples of emotions.

> An emotion is the way you interpret or describe a feeling.

*Note: you can find full lists of positive and negative emotions and their definitions in Appendix A and B at the back of this book.*

| Feeling | Possible emotions to choose | |
|---|---|---|
| Hunger or thirst | • Satisfaction | • Impatience |
| Bodily functions (eg. needing the toilet) | • Patience | • Pressure |
| Tiredness | • Peace | • Grumpiness |
| Creativity | • Amazement | • Anxiety |
| Grief | • Acceptance | • Self-pity |
| Love | • Trust | • Fear |
| Curiosity | • Embracing | • Doubt |
| Compassion | • Tenderness | • Frustration |
| Empathy | • Understanding | • Confusion |
| Gratitude | • Being nurtured | • Fragility |
| Aha! | • Confidence | • Insecurity |

In my 'Jules vs. the light switch' story earlier in the chapter, I didn't pay attention to my feeling of 'curiosity' as I was getting ready for bed. Because I ignored my feeling body, the emotion of frustration started to build and bubble away until it eventually boiled over.

If I'd paid attention to and honoured my feelings earlier, I could have noticed what was going on emotionally and chosen to change it.

The key is to remember that you always – *only always* – have a choice about your emotions.

That choice then becomes your key to creating an emotionally happy home in which you can feel 'light' regardless of what's happening with your emotions.

And that, in turn, is because you can choose your emotions and follow your feelings wisely.

## You already have everything you need

Another wonderful thing about the practices and principles of an emotionally happy home is that you know everything you need is available to you.

You don't need anyone else to do any specific thing – or be any specific way – for you to be emotionally happy. You realise at a soul level that you have something unique to contribute to the planet – and so does everyone else in your family and childhood family. And you know beyond knowing that everything you need will simply show up exactly when you need it, often in the most amazing ways.

> You don't need anyone else to do any specific thing – or be any specific way – for you to be emotionally happy.

Your emotions are your guide to this synchronicity and flow. For example, my 'Jules vs. the light switch' story didn't stop after I realised I had to apologise to my daughter…

### My story: Jules vs. the light switch – Part 2

Once I realised I had a mess to clean up, the first thing I did was to have an uncomfortable conversation with my daughter. In it, I owned my bad behaviour, apologised for it and told her what had been going on for me.

Because I've brought my kids up in an emotionally happy home culture, she didn't feel as though I was blaming her for my emotions. That meant I felt safe exploring them, which led to a startling insight.

I realised that my stress actually had nothing to do with the lights being left on. Instead, I'd been feeling sorry for myself because both of my kids had partners to share their lives with… and there I was, going to sleep alone. I also realised that I'd been running a story that said I wasn't enough on my own – that I needed a partner to complete me.

I decided that rather than stewing in the shame of having reacted badly, I'd take myself out for a coffee at one of my favourite cafes. It's something I love doing, and it helps to remind me that I'm absolutely enough in myself.

Then, when I got home, I asked myself what I most wanted to do at that point. I decided I wanted to tackle tidying up the garden – something I'd been making into a *huge* job in my mind and putting off for weeks. At that point, I had another flash of insight. I'd been making it so big because I had a story that 'I need a partner to help me with it'.

So I firmly reminded myself that I already had everything I needed and invited my kids and their partners to help. Between the five of us, we got the job done faster than I thought possible. And we had so much fun and experienced so much love and connection doing it too.

(I even got the satisfaction and delight of watching my kids practising some emotional hygiene principles while they worked!)

As I look back over this story, I realise that things would have gone very differently before I understood the principles of an emotionally happy home.

- I probably would have felt so ashamed and 'wrong' for having reacted badly that I would have been afraid to apologise to my daughter.

- If that conversation hadn't happened, I could have potentially damaged the loving, trusting relationship I have with her.

- If the conversation hadn't happened, I'd also never have had the flash of insight that everything stemmed from the unconscious conditioning that 'I'm incomplete without a partner'.

- If I hadn't had that insight, the feeling could have persisted and made me feel grumpy and irritable for weeks – maybe even months – before I dealt with it.

- If I hadn't dealt with it, I'd probably still be struggling to get the garden done – not to mention that I'd have missed out on some wonderful time bonding with my kids.

- If I hadn't dealt with it, I'd also still have a story that I wasn't enough and 'needed' a partner.

But because I DID have the conversation, explored my emotions and listened to my feelings, I could update my story to a better one. I could update it to 'I'm enough as I am right now. I have what I need when I need it. A partner will show up at the exact right moment if they're meant to'.

So while my 'reacting badly' felt awful in the moment, it truly led to some important insights. It also led to some wonderful moments of closeness with my kids.

That's the power of an emotionally happy home.

> 'Reacting badly' can feel awful in the moment, but it can truly lead to important insights.

*Life is a challenge... meet it! Life is a dream... realise it! Life is a game... play it! Life is love... enjoy it!*

– Sathya Sai Baba

## ☑ Chapter 1 Exercise

Grab your journal and pen, and find a quiet, comfortable place to sit, preferably at home. If you feel like it, you can also make a cup of tea and a plate of healthy snacks to nibble on. Let's make this fun!

Start by writing the date, and then read through the questions below. Then, one by one, answer them as candidly and clearly as possible.

Tune into your heart and higher self as you write, and don't hold back.

Let's go!

1. So far, what are your favourite things about an emotionally happy home culture?

2. Using a scale from 1 to 10 (1 being not much and 10 being very much) how aware are you of what you emotionally feel in your home?

3. What's the most common negative emotion you feel at home? Check the list of possible negative emotions and their definitions in Appendix A if you need inspiration. If you're still unsure, ask the others in your home. They'll know. ☺

4. Now that you know that emotions are a choice, what would you like to choose to emotionally feel instead of the emotion in Question 3?

   Refer to the list of positive emotions and their definitions in Appendix B for suggestions if you need to.

5. Do you believe that it's possible to choose and feel that positive emotion?

   - If yes, great! Choose it again and again over the next few days by saying,

     "Body, I now choose to feel [desired emotion] instead of [unpleasant emotion]."

     Notice how it gets easier each time, and notice the differences that choice makes.

- If not, repeat the affirmation below over the next two days.

    "I believe it's possible to change my emotional state."

    Then, after two days, repeat the question above.

6. From the list of feelings earlier in the chapter, what's one you'd love to be aware of undeniably feeling when it finds you?

7. To activate your awareness of this feeling, repeat the sentence below out loud for two days.

    "Body, show me when the feeling of [xxxx] finds me."

## Chapter 1 Summary

1. An emotionally happy home is one in which everyone honours and takes responsibility for their emotions.

2. Living in an emotionally happy home has many benefits, including making everyone feel safer, healthier, braver, more creative and more abundant.

3. The two core skills you need to master to create and maintain an emotionally happy home are managing emotional stress and practising emotional hygiene.

4. You won't get it right 100% of the time: there's always something more to learn.

5. Feelings and emotions are very different, and they communicate different information.

6. You already have everything you need to create an emotionally happy home and an emotionally happy life.

CHAPTER 2

# Emotionally Happy Homes Basics

## Before we go any further...

To explain how emotionally happy homes work at a grassroots level, I'll first need to define some concepts that might be new to you.

Sometimes, that will mean introducing you to a completely new term. Other times, it might mean introducing a new meaning for a term you already know. Either way, it's important to ensure we're both on the same page about my meaning in the rest of this book.

To help me explain each term in practice, I'd like to tell you about a real-life case study from one of my clients. Let's call her 'Susan' – although of course that's not her real name. Susan's experience was one I'd heard before from many, many other clients.

Here's what was going on in her life that kept her home from being emotionally happy...

## Susan's story: why can't I feel good about my life right now?

Susan and her husband Steve (also not his real name) came to see me because they both felt miserable at home.

On the surface, everything seemed great in Susan's life. She had a great relationship, great kids and a great job. In fact, she had everything you'd think she'd need to create a great home life. But in reality, below the surface, Susan was deeply unhappy with the way aspects of her life had unfolded.

While Susan herself wasn't consciously aware of that deep-seated unhappiness, it was abundantly obvious to Steve and the kids. It came out in the way she obsessed about the negatives of any situation. Steve could do ten things right and one wrong, and she'd focus straight in on whatever he'd done wrong. And even if she bit her tongue and didn't say a word, her displeasure was clear in her frustrated sighs, irritated gestures and other non-verbal signals.

It got to the point where he and the kids almost felt scared of her disapproval. Her relationship and her home were both in jeopardy.

As Susan and I worked together, it became obvious that her conditioning – both ancestral and personal – had taught her that she needed to strive for everything. If something was wrong, the only response that made sense to her was to do more, work harder and push more determinedly to fix it.

Nobody had ever taught her that real answers usually lie within – often only appearing when you stop 'doing' and start listening instead. So, with a little guidance, Susan started to explore what was really going on for her.

It took a while, but eventually, Susan was ready to acknowledge some difficult truths about what made her happy. She admitted to herself that her constant 'doing' had exhausted her and that she just wanted more time and space in her life for self-care activities.

In particular, she really wanted to reduce her work hours and go part-time at her job. She also wanted to stop dedicating her Saturday mornings to her sons' rugby games.

Unfortunately, Susan insisted, neither of those things could be changed. Steve *depended* on her to earn the money her job brought into their home. If she reduced her work hours, he'd be angry and disappointed with her. He might even leave her!

As for the Saturday morning rugby game, well, Steve had always been a rugby player. The boys wanted to follow in their father's footsteps, so she was sure that was non-negotiable too.

As the two of us worked together, however, Susan began to examine her assumptions. And as I introduced her to some of the concepts in this chapter, she started to realise that what she wanted might be less impossible than she'd assumed.

## Ancestral conditioning

The first concept I want to introduce you to in Susan's story is the idea of ancestral conditioning.

*Note: if you've always thought about the world in a logical, linear way, this concept might be a little challenging for you.*

*If so, I'm going to invite you to put any doubts to one side, at least until you finish reading this book. You can always pick them back up again afterwards! I also want to reassure you that you don't need to believe in this concept 100% for the rest of the book to work. You do, however, need to not keep getting 'stuck' in any doubts and letting them derail you as you read.*

'Ancestral conditioning' is simply the idea that the thoughts, beliefs and assumptions that lead to unconscious behaviours come from more than just your own personal experiences. As a child, everything you watch your parents go through and all the unconscious and conscious stories

> 'Ancestral conditioning' is simply the idea that the thoughts, beliefs and assumptions that lead to unconscious behaviours come from more than just your own personal experiences.

you hear about your grandparents and great-grandparents experiencing leave their mark.

When Susan looked back through her own childhood family history, she found two elements of ancestral conditioning at work: one from her great-grandmother and one from her parents. The more she explored, the more she realised that both had played dramatic roles in how she assumed Steve would view her need for more time to herself.

First, she looked at the overwhelmingly busy life her great-grandmother had led. This ancestor, Susan discovered, had birthed 16 children. Further, she'd had to raise and care for all those children on her own, with almost no help available to her.

Life had been hard for Susan's great-grandmother. The woman had barely ever had a moment to herself. Perhaps unsurprisingly, she'd developed a pattern of constant complaining and negativity. After all, if everything in the environment around her wasn't perfect, she probably feared her entire *life* would break down.

So Susan's great-grandmother had raised being critical to an art form.

Next, Susan looked at the relationship example her parents had set. She remembered hearing that her mother had once had a hairdressing career that she'd loved. As soon as her mum had become pregnant, though, Susan's father pressured her to give it up so she could look after their children. However, this choice wasn't enough for him: he'd ended up cheating on her and starting an affair with another woman.

So with these examples in her childhood family history, it was almost inevitable that Susan would come to unconsciously believe that:

- if everything in her life wasn't perfect, it would all fall apart
- she had to do everything on her own and couldn't ever ask for help
- if she didn't meet all of Steve's expectations, he'd leave her – just the way she'd seen her father do to her mother.

Realising that some of her deep, hidden subconscious beliefs and assumptions came from her ancestral lineage wasn't a magic wand that immediately changed them.

It was, however, an essential first step.

## Your emotional and feeling bodies

When you hear the word 'body', you probably think of the physical collection of systems, cells and organs that lets you interact with the world around you. But your physical body is just *one* of the types of bodies you have. Two others are your emotional body and your feeling body.

These are both energetic, interrelated, non-physical bodies, which – if you listen to them – can connect you with an immense amount of wisdom. Let's look at them each in turn.

### Your feeling body

Your feeling body's role is to sustain, nurture and nourish you. To do this, it provides information that can keep you feeling light and flowing in the current of life. That information comes directly from your heart and higher self.

> Your feeling body's role is to sustain, nurture and nourish you.

Your feeling body's messages will keep you feeling healthy and balanced. Listening to them always supports the bigger picture. It's like being on a mountain and having a guide who tells you what to wear to stay comfortable in the approaching weather.

For example, if your 'bigger picture' is that you need rest and rejuvenation, you'll experience a sense of tiredness from your feeling body. If you meet your need for rest, you'll feel a sense of being soothed and lifted out of the sense of tiredness.

So meet the messages from your feeling body with a smile, just like you'd meet a visitor to your house.

In Susan's case, however, her unresolved emotions stopped her from sensing her feeling body. That, in turn, kept her stuck in those negative emotions.

You'll know a message originates in your feeling body if you feel open to a wide range of possibilities to soothe it. For example, if you feel tired, you'll realise that you have several options available to satisfy your need for rest. These could include:

- a ten-minute power nap
- moving to a different room to meditate
- going for a gentle walk in nature
- stopping completely for the day and having a super early night.

All of these options – and more – are possible when the message that comes from your feeling body is still a gentle, intuitive one. If you ignore what your feeling body is telling you, however, the emotional messages will grow less gentle over time (more about this later in the chapter). If you *keep* ignoring the messages, you'll end up a slave not only to your negative emotions but to their associated patterns and programs as well.

## Your emotional body

Your emotional body's role is to let you know whether you're acting in alignment with your heart and higher self. It's like a kind of spiritual GPS, guiding you to walk the path your heart and higher self has set for you.

When your actions, thoughts or beliefs are out of alignment with your heart and higher self, you'll experience a sense of suffering from your emotional body. And unlike with the sensation in your feeling body that you want to soothe, you'll find yourself feeling emotionally wobbly and stuck in negative behaviours.

> Your emotional body's role is to let you know whether you're acting in alignment with your heart and higher self.

In contrast to your feeling body, your emotional body isn't open to multiple possibilities. It's limited to assuming that circumstances around you will always remain as they are right now. So your emotional body insists that the outside experience has to either change or go away for you to be happy.

In the example above, you might feel different emotions about the feeling of tiredness. You might feel grumpy – as though you 'shouldn't' be tired. Or you could feel peaceful and accept the feeling, recognising that you're only tired because you *need* to rest.

The first option makes it difficult to soothe your tiredness by resting, while the second makes it easy.

In Susan's case, the messages from her emotional body came in the form of obsessing about the negatives in any situation and being hypercritical. Only once her emotional body felt safe (when she stopped living in terror of Steve leaving her) could she start soothing her feeling body.

Luckily, as we discussed in the previous chapter, you can always – *only always* – with practice choose which emotion you want to feel. So over time, if you're experiencing an emotion you don't want, you can learn to quickly transform it into something that feels more pleasant.

## A quick warning about choosing your emotions

It's essential to know that your emotional body NEVER tries to get your attention without a good reason. Remember: its role is to tell you that something you're doing, thinking or believing is out of alignment with your heart and higher self.

So if you simply 'choose a different emotion' while ignoring whatever created the original one, your emotional body will just keep trying to get your attention. Repeatedly.

As it does, its messages will get louder and more insistent each time. They'll start as a gentle whisper and work their way up to a harsh slap in the face. Eventually, you'll start experiencing difficulties in your external life – in your relationships and/or in your physical and mental health.

In Susan's example, she developed several health issues, including a stiff neck, because she kept ignoring what her emotional wobbles (see below) were saying.

## Self-awareness

The next concept I want to explore with you is self-awareness: the quality of being consciously aware of what's emotionally going on within you.

This essential skill underlies every aspect of your work to make your home emotionally happy. It's the quality that empowers you to consciously choose to act, rather than unconsciously react (more about this distinction on the next page).

So why is self-awareness so critical to manage emotional stress and practise emotional hygiene? There are three key reasons:

> Self-awareness is the quality of being consciously aware of what's emotionally going on within you.

1. **Until you're aware of your ancestral conditioning, you can't see where it affects your patterns of thoughts and beliefs.**

    Consciously recognising patterns in the people who've gone before you almost always makes those patterns far easier to recognise within yourself.

    For example, Susan needed to become consciously aware of her great-grandmother's hypercritical complaining and her mother's fear of abandonment before she could see those patterns in herself.

2. **Unless you're consciously aware of the messages your emotional and feeling bodies are communicating, you can't act on them.**

    Until you're clear about what sensation you're actually feeling, you can't soothe it. Until you recognise the emotion you're actually experiencing, you can't transform it. And in both cases, you can't access the wisdom in each emotion or feeling until you're aware that it exists.

3. **The more self-aware you become, the safer you feel when other people 'act as your eyes'.**

    Self-awareness helps you to understand that other people often see you far more clearly than you see yourself, especially when you're in the thick of an emotional reaction.

    Without self-awareness, any loving feedback they give you about your reaction can feel like an attack – an accusation that you're doing something wrong. When you're self-aware, however, that same feedback becomes useful, valuable information about something you need to pay attention to.

That means developing self-awareness becomes a way to create more love within yourself, and more closeness and intimacy within your relationships.

## Self-awareness gives you a choice in how you'll respond

Throughout this book, I regularly contrast consciously choosing how you'll respond to a situation with simply reacting to it.

Without self-awareness, you can only react. When a trigger occurs (more on this term later in the chapter), you can only unconsciously, reflexively respond to it. I talk about 'reactions' and 'reactive behaviours' interchangeably in this book, and in Appendix C, you'll find a list of common reactive behaviours.

With self-awareness, however, you can consider your response. You can take the time to check in with your heart and higher self to see what they have to say, via your feeling body. And when you're ready, you can choose to act – or to *not* act – in a way that incorporates their wisdom and guidance.

Before Susan and I started working together, almost everything in her life was a reaction. She encountered trigger after trigger, experienced the associated emotions and reacted automatically. Sometimes, her reaction involved blaming or criticising Steve or the kids. Other times it involved drowning in her fears of being left alone. Yet other times it involved jumping to conclusions about what could and couldn't change in her life.

Only once she developed some self-awareness could she finally explore other, more constructive ways to respond to each trigger.

## Your self-awareness needs to be specific

Imagine you've just cut your finger in the kitchen. It's not a major drama, because you know your body can automatically heal that cut. However, it can *only* do so if it delivers exactly the right nutrients and healing factors to the exact site of the cut. Sending the wrong compounds to the cut or just generally pumping out more of them across your entire body won't do much to heal the injury.

Healing emotional wounds is no different. It requires the same level of self-awareness precision. You need to know exactly what's triggering your emotional reaction. You also need to understand what to 'send to that site' in terms of actions to take once you become aware of your reaction.

If you just try to develop general self-awareness, you'll never truly recognise what's going on. That, in turn, will leave you powerless to change anything.

## Curiosity and self-awareness

The path to self-awareness is always – *only always* – through the feeling of curiosity. If you have a strong emotion, don't assume you know what's behind it. Instead, get curious. Ask your heart what's going on.

> The path to self-awareness is always – *only always* – through the feeling of curiosity.

If, for example, you're emotionally feeling lonely and you're not sure why, try saying out loud,

> "Heart, what's behind this emotion of loneliness that I'm experiencing right now?"

After asking this question, let yourself become very still and quiet. Perhaps use the emotional shower technique in Chapter 6. Then allow the awareness of what's truly going on to just 'drop in'. Your body WILL supply that awareness if you let it – every single time.

Getting curious can create:

- closer connection with yourself
- closer connection and togetherness within your relationships
- greater internal peace
- more health, vitality and energy
- clearer mental focus.

It can also help you to:

- get clearer on who you really are and confidently express it
- make choices from your heart and act on them creatively
- hear your intuition more accurately
- communicate more consciously.

… and *so much* more!

Getting curious helped Susan to become aware that her emotional wobbles, frustration and irritation had absolutely nothing to do with Steve or the kids. Nor did they have anything to do with the state of the house or who'd left what out on the bench. Instead, they sprang from her need for more rest and space in her life.

Additionally, getting curious allowed Susan to let Steve 'be her eyes' whenever she unconsciously sighed in frustration or tossed her head in annoyance. It allowed her to hear him saying, "Hey babe, did you notice that you just complained again there?" as useful information instead of as an attack.

Only once she knew these things could she do anything about them.

## Emotional triggers and wobbles

Next, let's explore how your emotional body talks to you when you're not paying attention. Most often, it will communicate through reactions that I like to call 'wobbles'.

I use the term 'wobble' because it's a wonderfully general word that can cover a multitude of negative emotions. It incorporates emotions that range from fear to worry to irritation to loneliness to anger and everything in between.

I love the word because it brings a sense of lightness to experiences that could otherwise feel crushingly heavy. I also love it because it can help to identify and name an emotional state without attaching any blame or judgement to it.

**A wobble is any emotional reaction that tells you you're out of alignment with your heart and higher self.**

> A wobble is any emotional reaction that tells you you're out of alignment with your heart and higher self.

That means any wobble you experience contains important information and is well worth paying attention to. Remember: if you don't pay attention, your emotional body will just keep repeating its messages, getting louder and probably more painful each time!

Susan's wobbles were the frustration and annoyance she felt when things around the house weren't done to her liking. They were also the exhaustion and overwhelm she experienced as she strove to constantly do, do, do, and fix the things she saw as 'wrong'. Plus, of course, they were the terror she felt about the possibility of Steve leaving her.

**A trigger is any outside situation or event that leads to you experiencing a wobble.**

Perhaps your trigger is getting stuck in rush hour traffic. Maybe it's your boss's tone of voice when they speak to you. It might be a particular behaviour that drives you crazy in one of your kids. Regardless, you'll know something is a trigger for you if you find yourself blaming it for the negative emotion you feel.

In Susan's case, her trigger was seeing things in the house that weren't to her liking. Perhaps Steve hadn't finished putting the laundry away or one of her sons had left toast crumbs on the bench after breakfast. Before she developed more self-awareness, she simply assumed that these things MADE her annoyed.

Of course, in the three-part agreement we talked about in Chapter 1, we agreed that nothing and nobody is responsible for your emotions but you. We also agreed that every emotion *only always* has an important message for you that you're out of alignment with your heart in some way.

So even though you might feel a trigger is responsible for your anger or fear or frustration, the reality is very different. The reality is that any trigger gives you valuable information (through your emotional wobble) about something that needs attention in your life.

So learn to see wobbles and the triggers that cause them as your friends.

Without them, you'd never be able to develop either spiritual intelligence or emotional maturity.

## Spiritual intelligence and emotional maturity

The final terms I want to talk about in this chapter are spiritual intelligence and emotional maturity. These concepts place the idea of an emotionally happy home in a broader context than just the sense of peace you experience within your own four walls.

Don't misunderstand me: what you experience at home absolutely IS important. That experience flows from within your four walls outward to every other aspect of your life. But it's not where the benefits of emotional maturity – a term I use to encompass developing self-awareness and accepting total responsibility for emotional hygiene – end.

Instead, the greatest benefit of cultivating emotional maturity is that it leads to developing deeper spiritual intelligence.

When I talk about spiritual intelligence, I'm referring to concepts that ancient cultures have been exploring and refining for millennia. In particular, I'm referring to the inner peace that comes from realising that you already have everything you need available to you.

> The greatest benefit of cultivating emotional maturity is that it leads to developing deeper spiritual intelligence.

When we recognise this deeper spiritual truth, life suddenly becomes so much easier. We remember that we're complete in ourselves, and we can allow OTHER people to be complete in themselves as well. We don't need anyone else to be anything other than what they already are or do anything other than what they already do.

When we accept this truth, we find ourselves developing a whole different relationship with the world – one based on what we can contribute instead of what we can get. For example, I've discovered that *my* contribution is to teach others how to transform, understand and manage their emotional stress. In doing this, they naturally begin to practise the spiritual laws and guidelines that resonate for them daily with others in their homes.

And if enough people do this, I truly believe it will evolve our planet and the human race.

The fundamental concepts of completeness and contribution come cloaked in a range of different details. Each set of details can help you to understand the core concepts from a different perspective. The easiest way to explore which set of details work best for you is to find mentors who resonate for you and learn from them.

For example, some of the mentors I've been drawn to have included:

- Gregg Braden
- Bruce Lipton
- Bashar
- Kryon
- Shirley MacLaine
- Shakti Gawain
- Sathya Sai Baba
- Louise Hay
- Abraham Hicks
- My own heart and higher self.

You may feel drawn to others; if so, that's totally OK. You'll know what's right for you, so trust wherever your heart leads you.

## Susan's story: the happy ending

After learning how the basic emotionally happy homes concepts applied in Susan and Steve's life, you might be interested in knowing how things turned out for their family.

First, with some self-awareness, Susan realised just how much her reactive emotional behaviours negatively affected Steve and the kids. She also recognised what lay beneath those behaviours – the desire for more time and space for herself.

A little *more* self-awareness helped her to realise that her assumptions about her desires being impossible were just that – assumptions. She acknowledged that Steve loved her and was very, very unlikely to leave her if she admitted she wanted to change something in their relationship.

Just on the off-chance that he did leave her, however, a little spiritual intelligence helped her to realise that she was complete in herself. That meant she felt a deep, peaceful sense of total acceptance that she could survive and thrive on her own.

So, after a few weeks and a LOT of support, she gathered up her courage and talked to Steve. She broached the idea of working part-time and of the boys giving up their Saturday morning rugby, certain that Steve would object strongly to both suggestions.

Instead, to her surprise, Steve was delighted. He'd actually been longing to cut back on his work hours too – and they quickly realised that they could easily afford to both go part-time. As for the Saturday morning rugby game, Steve told her that the boys didn't actually *enjoy* playing. They only went every week because 'Mum thinks it's important', and he had no desire to force them to continue.

So because Susan was willing to be a leader and act with emotional maturity, EVERYONE in her home benefited.

## ☑ Chapter 2 Exercise

The questions below will help you to begin connecting with, or deepening your connection with, your emotional body. They'll also help you to awaken, explore and increase your self-awareness.

Start by stating out loud,

> "Body, I allow any awareness to come through that supports my growth and expansion as I answer these questions."

Then grab your journal and pen, and perhaps another drink or snack.

Finally, read each question below slowly and write down your answers.

As you do, tune into whatever emotions you feel coming up, and observe any distracting thoughts that arise or any physical reactions you notice.

Write those all down as well.

1. What are your emotionally happiest times at home? Who are they with?

2. What are your emotional triggers at home? What experiences or people make you emotionally wobbly?

3. What's your most common emotional wobble from those triggers? Examples might include overwhelm, feeling pressured, dullness, numbness, anger, resentment, frustration, shutting down, grumpiness, self-pity, depression or anxiety.

4. What's the history of your most common emotional wobbles? For example:

   - Have they always been there?
   - Can you identify any of them from your childhood?
   - Did you also see any of them in a parent or grandparent?

5. What positive emotion would you like to replace your most common emotional wobble with? See Appendix B for possible examples to choose from.

## Chapter 2 Summary

1. Your current patterns of beliefs, thoughts and behaviours are based on more than just your own personal experiences.

2. Your emotional and feeling bodies both provide valuable information that your conscious mind can't access on its own.

3. Self-awareness is the key to choosing how to respond to any given trigger, and the feeling of curiosity is the key to self-awareness.

4. An emotional wobble is any negative emotional reaction that occurs in response to an external trigger.

5. While the peace and happiness that result from an emotionally happy home are wonderful, the biggest benefit is the ability to develop spiritual intelligence and emotional maturity.

CHAPTER 3

# Understanding Emotions in Depth

## Emotions: a quick recap

Back in Chapter 1, we talked briefly about the importance of emotions. We described them as a source of clear internal guidance – a bit like an inner GPS.

We also discussed the idea that emotions tell you when your thoughts, beliefs or actions are out of alignment with your heart and higher self. And, finally, we started to talk about the difference between feelings and emotions.

Then, in Chapter 2, I introduced you to your emotional and feeling bodies, along with the concepts of emotional triggers and wobbles. You also learnt about the importance of self-awareness and curiosity when it comes to working with emotions.

Now it's time to dive much deeper into what emotions are, how they support you and what you need to know to work with them. But first, another real-life story…

## Lucy's story: the power of intense emotions

When Lucy (also not her real name) first came to see me, she was panicking.

She'd discovered a large lump in one breast that she was terrified to get her doctor to check. She'd watched her grandmother go through a long, difficult battle with cancer, and she couldn't see *any* other explanation as realistic apart from cancer.

At the same time, something deep down inside her believed that she could heal the lump on her own. That meant she felt hugely conflicted. One part of her said she had the power to heal it, while everything else was convinced she'd die the same horrible way her grandmother had.

As we talked, it became clear that Lucy was extremely emotional, and she'd been taught to see this as an immense character flaw. She tried her hardest to dampen down her emotions, but her high sensitivity drove all of her family, friends and workmates crazy. And when her emotional wobbles hit, they overwhelmed her and everyone around her like a whirlwind.

So, before we did anything else together, I suggested that Lucy needed to do two things:

1. She needed to talk to her doctor and get the lump checked. But she had to approach the conversation from a place of curiosity, instead of one of fear. And she needed to view medical professionals as potential allies, instead of people to be scared of.

2. She also needed to start seeing her emotions as a source of power and healing energy. To help with this, I asked her to imagine her emotions as a beautiful crystal wand that she could focus on the lump. The more intense her emotions felt, the stronger the healing energy would be.

Then, once she'd done these things, we could start working together on healing her lump – whatever it turned out to be – at the deepest possible level.

Lucy agreed and went to see her doctor, who told her that the lump was the size of a 50-cent piece and wanted to immediately biopsy it.

Lucy replied that she'd like to try healing it herself first and asked for six weeks to work on it with me. The doctor reluctantly agreed, and Lucy made an appointment to check in again in six weeks' time.

After that, Lucy and I started working together twice a week in an extremely intense process that she nicknamed 'energetic chemo'. She began to connect with her energetic and feeling bodies and allow the wisdom from her heart and higher self to flow through. (You'll find out more about what we did and what she learnt later in the chapter.)

Six weeks later, she went back to see her doctor as agreed. And to everyone's surprise – well, everyone except for Lucy and me – the lump had completely gone. It was as though it had never been there.

Her story is a testament to the power of emotions to heal on a physical level.

## The benefits of your emotions

If, like Lucy, you're used to experiencing your emotions as uncomfortable, uncontrollable and inconvenient, it can be hard to see them as good things.

Yes, sure, 'positive' emotions like happiness, contentment, optimism and satisfaction feel good and make our lives better when we experience them. But what about the so-called 'negative' ones? What about fear, anxiety, worry, anger and frustration – the ones I collectively call 'emotional wobbles'? Wouldn't we all be better off if we could just cut *those* emotions out of our lives completely?

NO!

A thousand times no, in fact.

If you take nothing else from reading this chapter, I want you to take the idea that ALL emotions are beneficial. Strong emotions may not feel

> An emotion tells you whether your thoughts, beliefs or actions are in alignment with your heart and higher self.

wonderful in the moment, but they always – *only always* – have immense benefits. Here's what I mean…

## Emotions offer infallible guidance

We started talking about the guidance your emotions can provide in Chapter 1. To understand how this works, it helps to go back to the basic definition of an emotion:

An emotion tells you whether your thoughts, beliefs or actions are in alignment with your heart and higher self.

- If a belief, thought or action creates a positive-feeling emotion, you know without a doubt that it's aligned with your heart and higher self.
- If it creates a negative-feeling emotion, however, you know SOMETHING about that thought, belief or action is out of alignment with your heart and higher self.

And regardless of whether an emotion feels positive or negative, the more intense it is, the stronger its power to heal or create change in your life.

Here's how that played out in Lucy's life…

### Lucy's story: the wisdom within emotions

As Lucy and I worked together, we explored more of the parallels between her life and her grandmother's.

One of the first words she used to describe her grandmother to me was 'hoarder'. This was something that Lucy insisted she'd never allow herself to be. She'd recognised early in her life that holding on to things she really needed to let go of was an issue, so she'd actively worked on this.

In her life now, she liked a minimalist aesthetic. She kept everything spotlessly clean, uncluttered and tidy in her life and home. So as far as her conscious mind was concerned, she'd dealt with the hoarding instinct. It was no longer an issue.

However, as she learnt how to actively ask her feeling and emotional bodies for awareness, and then listen to their guidance, she had a flash of insight. Her physical environment might be neat, clean and ordered... but her digital environment was something else entirely.

Shocked, she realised that she couldn't remember the last time she'd decluttered the hard drive on her computer. She had a jumbled, unorganised collection of thousands of files on there that dated back years, if not decades. And the energy of that disorganisation was keeping her stuck and blocked in her life.

Now, it might not sound like much for someone to commit to cleaning out and organising a folder of computer files. But for Lucy, the task had an enormous amount of stuck emotional energy attached to it. In fact, it was so huge and overwhelming that for her it was the equivalent of someone else giving up an addiction like smoking or alcohol.

Once she actively started to declutter, she became aware that it was triggering the same emotional wobble of overwhelm in her that it had in her grandmother. As she continued to take action, however, the emotions gradually grew less overwhelming.

And everything else in her life started to flow more smoothly as well – including her health.

Remember that your heart and higher self both always – *only always* – have your best interests at heart. They also *only always* know the best actions to take to achieve those interests. And they have the answers to any questions that come up for you.

> Your heart and higher self both always – *only always* – have your best interests at heart.

Unfortunately, they communicate their wisdom in a language that you've probably been taught from an early age to ignore – the language of emotions. And, as we discussed in Chapter 2, they might start off communicating in a quiet whisper of an emotion. If you keep ignoring them, however, they'll get louder and more insistent.

Eventually, they'll start to yell.

Ironically, the very fact that Lucy kept trying to push down emotions she'd been taught were 'bad' made them even more intense and all-engulfing. Once she started listening to them, though, they became far more manageable and less devastating.

## Emotions can literally change your reality

One definition I've heard of emotions is 'energy in motion'.

The energy that makes up an emotion is the same energy that gives vitality and life to *everything* in our universe. That energy may feel positive or negative, based on your definition of the experience, but it's fundamentally neutral. And this means you can use it in any way you want to, once you learn how.

When I talk about 'free energy' in this book, that's the kind of energy I mean.

As I helped Lucy to discover, the stronger and more intense your emotions are, the more energy they carry. So if you can focus that energy, you can *use* it to create natural momentum that helps you make changes in your life.

However, all too often, when we want to change something in our lives, we try to force it. We push. If that doesn't work, we just push harder. Then we wonder why we exhaust ourselves, while nothing ends up changing.

Focusing the energy of your emotions on creating a change is a very different approach. It allows you to create that change in a way that's aligned with your heart and higher self. It's like smoothly, effortlessly surfing a wave into shore, instead of trying to fight the ocean's current. (Spoiler alert: the ocean will *only always* win!)

Here's how that natural momentum showed up for Lucy…

## Lucy's story: how emotion can create natural momentum for change

Another insight that bubbled to the surface as Lucy and I worked together was, quite simply, that she was feeling unfulfilled in her work life.

Deep down, Lucy realised, she was a strongly ambitious woman. She'd always felt a calling to work with young women and help them to connect with their creativity. She'd once dreamed of taking that calling into the national – perhaps even international – arena.

But… somewhere along the way, she'd absorbed the message that creating that kind of business *wasn't* what a good woman did. It certainly wasn't what an extremely emotional woman did!

Instead, she'd learnt that a good woman only focused on her family – supporting and nurturing her children and husband. It wasn't her job to have big goals and ambitions. Her role was to help everyone else in her home achieve theirs, even at the cost of her own dreams.

Not, of course, that there's anything wrong with genuinely feeling called to fulfil a role as a supporter. But that's not where Lucy's heart and higher self were pointing her.

The intense emotions she felt in part reflected the misalignment between their calling and her beliefs about what she *should* do with her life.

Plus, even if she did decide to try following her heart's guidance, she had no idea where to start.

As we worked together to uncover these suppressed ambitions, Lucy also asked her higher self how she might take a first step towards achieving them. And again, the awareness she received from her body kept pointing her back to her digital hoarding habits. Perhaps, she wondered, if she organised and cleaned up those files, it would release whatever block was stopping her from seeing her next step?

So, drawing deeply on her courage and determination, Lucy went off to confront the mess of files on her computer.

A couple of days later, I got an excited phone call from her. Apparently, back when she'd been single, she'd written a vast amount of content about connecting with creativity that she'd completely forgotten about. There were entire volumes' worth of it sitting in the files she was clearing out – enough to create ebooks, workbooks and even a guided program.

This content, she realised, was her first step. All she had to do was organise it, publish it and then market it.

Over the next few months, after getting the all-clear from her doctor, that's exactly what she did. Quickly, she became known as the pre-eminent expert in her field.

It was a beautiful example of using natural momentum to create aligned change.

## Want a sense of how using emotional energy could work in your life?

Think about the biggest thing that's not working in your life right now – something you feel intensely emotional about. It might be:

- a diagnosed medical condition (or just a desire to feel better physically)
- the amount of money you're bringing into your home
- a job that feels stressful and unfulfilling
- the lack of any opportunity to use your creative gifts
- a damaged relationship that upsets you.

Take a moment to just tune into the depth of the emotion you feel about that issue. Can you feel the energy that emotion carries?

Now, can you imagine the power of harnessing that energy and using it to change the reality around that issue? Can you imagine it all changing smoothly and easily as you 'surf the wave' of natural momentum into the shore of the change you want?

That's exactly what Lucy did. And I promise you that – once you know what you're doing – you can do it too if you're willing to.

## The good news about intense negative-feeling emotions

Another benefit of intense negative-feeling emotions is the way they show us the power of duality. In other words, the deeper the negative-feeling emotion you actually experience, the higher the peaks of positive emotion you're capable of feeling.

Imagine a scale of intensity for stressful emotions like fear, anxiety, anger, etc. which runs from a Level 1 to a Level 10.

> The deeper the negative-feeling emotion you actually experience, the higher the peaks of positive emotion you're capable of feeling.

When you're at a Level 1 on this scale, you're just barely aware of a slight niggle. You actually have to be paying close attention in the first place to even notice it, so it's super easy to miss and even easier to ignore. At a Level 10, however, the emotion is all-consuming. You can't think, you can't reason and you certainly can't recognise the way that anything you do affects the people around you.

In Chapter 5, we're going to talk in much more detail about what each specific range in this emotional scale means and what to do when you're within it. For now, however, I just want you to think about the outer extremes of the scale: Levels 1 and 10.

Now, most of us have grown up believing – as Lucy did – that it's better to be a calm, easygoing person who never gets upset. In other words, the ideal is to stay as close to a Level 1 as possible.

At the same time, most of us are taught that happiness and gratitude are things we should strive for. So imagine that there's a similar scale for positive-feeling emotions. On this scale, Level 1 is being distantly aware of something slightly pleasant. Again, it's easy to miss if you're not paying close attention. And Level 10 is deep, all-encompassing cosmic bliss and rapture.

Most of us would agree – assuming we actually believe a Level 10 positive emotion is possible – that it's the place we'd want to hang out. But the truth is that there aren't two separate scales: one for negative-feeling emotions and one for positive-feeling ones. Instead, there's just a single scale of emotional intensity.

So if you're capable of feeling those deep, painful lows, you're *every bit* as capable of feeling the soaring, blissful highs.

It might take work, but you're capable of it.

## What if you don't feel emotional extremes?

If you're someone who simply doesn't seem to feel emotional extremes, I want to assure you that it's not because you're incapable of deep emotional feeling. Everyone is born with the capacity for intense emotional wobbles.

However, some of us learn very early on to push those emotions down hard. Eventually, we do it so well for so long that we forget we could ever do anything else. And on the surface, that can look as though Level 1 emotions are all we're capable of.

If this describes you, don't despair. The more curious you get about your Level 1 emotions, and the more attention you pay to them, the more you'll be able to access the power of other stronger emotional wobbles. This then allows you to easily access your feeling body and the wisdom in your heart and higher self.

Again, it might take work. But I promise you, it'll be worth it.

## A final note: you're never 'stuck' with an unpleasant emotion

The idea of working with emotions, especially if they're intense and painful, can be a scary one. So before I close out this chapter, I want to reassure you that you're never stuck with no alternative but to stay in an unpleasant emotion.

Here's why: we've talked already about the general difference between feelings and emotions. If you need a quick refresher, though, here it is:

- A feeling is an internal sensation that's undeniable, and it exists to sustain, nurture or nourish you.
- An emotion is the way that you interpret or describe the experience of that feeling, and it is negotiable.

That difference means that while you can't choose or change a feeling – at least, not without taking some action to create or soothe it – you can *only always* choose your emotion.

> You can learn from and work with your emotions, even the so-called negative ones, WITHOUT having to feel bad.

This distinction can be really hard to wrap your head around if you're used to confusing feelings and emotions. It can be even harder if, like Lucy, you've learnt to associate strong emotions and feelings with weakness and a lack of self-control.

The truth, however, is that you can learn from and work with your emotions, even the so-called negative ones, WITHOUT having to feel bad.

For example, let's say that you wake up one morning and notice you're feeling exhausted.

As you become aware of this tiredness, you might feel as though you only have two options:

- You can try to ignore the tiredness, push it down and focus on getting everything done in your life. This feels better in the moment and is what society often encourages us to do… but it invariably leads to problems later on.

- Or, alternatively, you can focus on the exhaustion and how much you dislike it. You can feel angry at yourself for going to bed late or resentful of whatever it was that kept you awake. And you can keep that negative reaction up all day until it's finally bedtime when you can let yourself rest.

But… what if those AREN'T your only options?

What if, instead of assuming your feeling of tiredness was inextricably bound up with the heavy emotions of anger and resentment, you asked your heart what you needed to do? What if you put your hand on your heart and said out loud,

> "Heart, I'm experiencing heavy emotions around my feeling of tiredness right now. What's the best thing I can do to feel lighter?"

As we discussed in the previous chapter, depending on your specific circumstances, the answer might bubble up to:

- take a ten-minute power nap
- shift some of the things on your task list until tomorrow
- cancel an appointment or meeting you had booked
- give yourself the day off completely.

Whatever the answer, I guarantee you that there will be a way for you to genuinely experience the tiredness *without* it feeling heavy and painful.

# Chapter 3 Exercises

**Exercise 1**

Begin to recognise the difference between your feelings and emotions.

For example, start with paying attention to the feeling of 'being tired' over the next day. Tiredness is easy to notice.

When you experience the feeling of being tired, acknowledge it out loud. Say,

> "Body, I'm sensing the feeling of tiredness. Thank you. I acknowledge this as a feeling. I know I'll tend to it soon and look forward to it. Meanwhile, I choose to be emotionally happy with this feeling."

Each time the feeling nudges you to tend to it, repeat the statement.

Practise this as often as you can.

It won't be long until you feel very empowered with this ability.

**Exercise 2**

I invite you to work with the belief that your emotions and your emotional body are your strength.

Say out loud,

**"I believe that my emotions and emotional body are my strength."**

Affirm this belief to yourself several times every day. I recommend saying it to yourself each time you walk into the bathroom, laundry or kitchen. This gives you a physical location anchor for the affirmation – a place that you'll usually find yourself in every day.

Write down this belief, and perhaps decorate the paper you've written on.

If you love colouring mandalas, dedicate one to this belief. Maybe get everyone in your home together and colour one each.

Then frame the mandala or other artwork, and put it somewhere visible so you can see it every day.

This belief will enhance your life beyond what you currently see as possible.

## Chapter 3 Summary

1. Emotions – especially strong emotions – are a source of strength and offer many benefits.

2. Your emotions are a source of infallible guidance from your heart and higher self.

3. You can use the energy of emotions to create massive changes in your everyday life and reality.

4. If you can feel intense negative emotions, it means you have the capacity to feel equally intense positive ones.

5. You're never stuck with a negative-feeling emotion: you can *only always* feel emotionally light around all your feelings.

CHAPTER 4

# Understanding Emotional Stress

## What is emotional stress?

Take a moment and a breath to be present.

You're about to learn all about emotional stress – what it is and how it affects you. In particular, you're going to learn how it affects the 'you' who shows up in your home and family.

In some ways, emotional stress is no different from emotional wobbles. Like an emotional wobble, emotional stress happens when your heart and higher self guide you to do one thing, and your beliefs, patterns, programs and conditioning say, "No."

And just as with emotional wobbles, the specific name you give your emotional stress doesn't matter. It might be insecurity, frustration, anger or fear. Regardless, what's *important* is that there's a message behind the emotion.

> The specific name you give your emotional stress doesn't matter.

But where emotional wobbles happen in the moment, emotional stress builds up gradually. If you consistently ignore or try to push down your emotional wobbles, they start to turn into emotional stress that gets stronger over time.

At the beginning, it might just feel subtle – perhaps a slight sense of confusion, distraction or unease. Sometimes at this level, it might even have signs that don't feel 'bad', and we'll talk about these in the next chapter. If you continue to ignore your stress, however, the signs will get harder and harder to ignore.

Unless you resolve and heal your emotional stress, it starts to affect – and infect – every part of both your life and the lives of the people around you. We'll go into more detail about how it does this, and what that can look like, later in this chapter.

The good news is that as you get more practice it becomes easier to spot and resolve emotional wobbles BEFORE they turn into emotional stress. And a wobble doesn't need to result from something huge and dramatic to be important either…

## My story: messages from emotional stress

A few days before editing this chapter, I came home from yoga and felt myself starting to wobble. Something felt as though it wasn't right, and I noticed my thoughts were getting increasingly negative.

The strongest, heaviest thought I could hear was that I was 'wrong'.

Initially, I wasn't sure where the emotions and thoughts were coming from. I knew they had to contain some kind of message, though. So as I stood in the shower with the hot water cascading down over me, I decided to ask my body.

To lift me out of the stress, I put my hand on my heart, tuned into my feeling body and said, "Come on, body. What do you have to say to me?"

Straight away, the feeling of gratitude came flooding into my awareness. This was my body's answer. There were so many things I had to feel grateful for, and I just wasn't acknowledging them.

I felt grateful for the way the process was unfolding with this book. I felt grateful for having managed to speak with my children every day that week. And I felt immensely grateful for having been able to practise yoga every day too.

So I took a moment to allow myself to really FEEL and receive that gratitude.

Once I was done, though, I sensed that something else was there too.

So I asked my feeling body, "OK, body. What *else* are you trying to tell me?"

This time, the answer came back as 'tired'.

Now, years ago, I would have ignored this feeling. After all, it was mid-morning on a Friday. Back then, my ego wouldn't have let me stop doing, doing, doing until 5pm at the earliest. I'd have demanded to know WHY I was feeling tired. I'd have seen it as further evidence of something being 'wrong' and probably something to feel guilty about.

I've learnt a lot since then, though. These days, I don't need to know *why* I have the feeling of tiredness. It's enough for me to know that my feeling body is suggesting I rest.

So, as I stood there in the shower, I reminded myself that I'd set my life and mindset up specifically so that I *could* stop and rest whenever I wanted to. I chose, in that moment, to feel peaceful about the tired feeling. And as I dried off and dressed afterwards, I knew I didn't need to do anything that day that I didn't want to.

Braced by that reminder, I made a pot of nutritious soup, sat down to enjoy a few Bashar videos and simply let myself recharge.

> Emotional stress can look different for everyone.

## How emotional stress can show up in your life

It's easy to assume you know how emotional stress looks when it shows up in your life. The reality, however, is that it can be different for everyone. Here are just a *few* of the possible signs and signals you might notice if you have unresolved emotional stress in your life.

### Physical signs

- poor sleep or restlessness
- illnesses, eg. viruses, cancers and other disorders
- back, neck or shoulder aches
- headaches, rashes and even warts
- tiredness for no valid reason
- excess hunger or stubborn weight
- addictions
- not liking how your body looks but doing nothing about it.

### Mental signs

- negative thoughts
- lots of repetitive negative stories in your head
- never feeling satisfied
- low self-esteem
- feeling fatalistic towards new or different experiences
- a sense of overwhelm
- confusion
- worries about money.

### Emotional signs

- emotional outbursts
- fear of stepping out of your comfort zone
- fear of telling the truth
- lack of personal self-care and motivation
- lack of natural momentum.

### Communication signs

- hearing yourself repeatedly complaining about the same things
- communication blocks
- inability to communicate clearly
- communicating repetitive stories and excuses to other people
- fear of speaking up
- fighting with someone else
- insecurities around being social
- resistance to being around members of your family or childhood family.

### Environmental signs

- disorganisation in your paperwork, housework or garden
- lack of money.

As you read through that list, you may notice that one (perhaps a few) of the signs appear in your life or home. Then, if you're like many people, your mind may immediately start to object to those things being signs of emotional stress.

Maybe you believe that disorganisation is simply a core part of who you are. Perhaps you're sure you're just naturally shy. Or maybe you have a difficult history with your childhood family that makes 'resistance to being around them' feel like a smart, self-caring response.

But I want you to know that you don't NEED to live with any of these things. You certainly don't need to live with the emotional stress they often signify.

> *"Circumstances don't matter, only state of being matters."*
> – Bashar

## How emotional stress can help you

The key to working with emotional stress is to realise that in and of itself, it's not a negative thing.

Yes, ignoring emotional stress has many negative effects, as you'll find out later in this chapter. However, in almost all circumstances, emotional stress can be a source of great insight and help. You could think of it as an indicator on a car. It simply shows you the direction you're currently going in, so you can make better, more informed choices.

> The key to working with emotional stress is to realise that in and of itself, it's not a negative thing.

Another metaphor I love to use for emotional stress is a beach-based one. Imagine that following the path of your heart is like swimming in a beautiful, calm ocean on a hot day. Emotional stress is like the lifeguards patrolling that beach. It puts up flags to show you where you can safely swim. It also points out where the dangerous rips are, and it warns you if there are sharks.

But emotional stress can do so much more than just help you to navigate your daily life. It can also be a tool that highlights fantastic opportunities to become more emotionally mature and spiritually intelligent. It can help you to recognise when you're stuck in your comfort zone, and support you as you update and evolve your limiting beliefs and conditioning.

In short, it can help you to become more of who you truly are.

And if you can view it this way and pay attention to it when it shows up in subtle ways, it can be *immensely* beneficial.

## Emotional stress can happen at any time

The next thing to be aware of is that emotional stress doesn't just happen when you're feeling bad. It can find you at any time – and it always has a message for you when it does.

> Emotional stress doesn't just happen when you're feeling bad.

As with an emotional wobble, it tells you that there's a conflict somewhere between your thoughts and beliefs, and your heart and higher self. So, for example:

- If your thoughts and beliefs are keeping you stuck in your comfort zone, emotional stress can help to nudge you back onto your path.

- Or, if you're on your path but your limiting beliefs are making you uncomfortable, emotional stress can help you to recognise the problem and finetune those beliefs.

This is one reason it's so important to pay attention to the subtle signs of emotional stress when they show up. Managing it at this level is so much easier than waiting until it builds up into something more dramatic.

## Emotional stress can also be passed from one person to another

There's one exception to the rule that emotional stress can benefit you. Sometimes, the emotional stress you experience isn't actually yours. You can pick it up – or pick up the beliefs that create it – from other people who are close to you.

This happens most commonly at home because of the close bonds between people who live together – especially in childhood families. Sometimes, it's like everyone in the house is passing an invisible, emotional stress energy ball back and forth around the room.

So, for example, imagine that your partner is feeling a lot of emotional stress. If you're not present and focused on your own journey, you'll probably end up taking on that stress yourself. I sometimes describe unresolved emotional stress as being like a virus: it can infect everyone around you!

In particular, because children often don't know what their own journey is yet, they'll take on the stress of adults around them. Emotional stress can even be passed down through your lineage from generation to generation.

This means that if you ignore unresolved stress around your childhood family and lineage, your children will end up taking it on. That can then have a multitude of negative effects as you'll see in the next section.

Most of us value knowing about any history of physical illness we might have in our families. We often don't realise that it's just as important, if not more so, to know our emotional childhood family history too.

That's why choosing to resolve and heal your stress not only makes *your* life better – it also frees up the lives of your children.

## Why you need to resolve emotional stress

When I talk about unresolved emotional stress having negative effects, I mean that it will eventually cause suffering of some sort in your life.

On its way, it will affect your home, workplace, finances, health, relationships, parenting, friendships, creativity and so much more. In fact, it will affect everyone you're in contact with, including your children, pets, family and friends.

Let's take a look at a few of the ways that unresolved emotional stress can affect your life.

### Physical effects

> Over time, unresolved emotional stress WILL start to show up physically in your body.

Over time, unresolved emotional stress WILL start to show up physically in your body.

It will develop into sickness and disease, making you more susceptible to viruses and other pathogens. It will directly infect your organs and your body, stealing and trapping the free energy from them that they need to function properly.

On top of this, it will completely sap your motivation to look after yourself, making you more vulnerable to disease and other health issues. It will even make you resist taking time off when you need it, ensuring that the only way to get the rest you need is to fall ill.

When you begin to manage and resolve your emotional stress, your organs will start to let go of the trapped energy and restore its flow. This, in turn, will help to restore *you* to full health, vitality, presence and consciousness.

I've seen so many cases of people being hospitalised with serious medical conditions that result from ignoring their emotional stress. I've seen unresolved stress – sometimes inherited from previous generations – manifest as heart attacks, strokes, Ross River fever, chronic fatigue and more.

I've also seen chronic conditions improve significantly when the person involved truly begins to work with their emotional stress. And I've seen people who have healed their emotional stress go on to take great care of themselves, realising that they didn't actually need to be sick to have a 'sick day'.

Of course, I always recommend speaking to a doctor or other medical professional if you're experiencing physical illness or health issues. But if you're already working with professionals and nothing's shifting, I strongly recommend exploring what's going on emotionally.

## Communication effects

Emotional stress also affects your ability to communicate with everyone else in your home.

This is partly because when something triggers emotional stress for you, you tend to mentally regress back to the age you were when that thing first triggered you. So you might be 40 years old now, but suddenly find yourself acting and feeling like a 4-year-old. This affects how you think and communicate, as well as your ability to speak up for yourself.

Note that when I use the word 'trigger' there, I don't necessarily mean you'll experience the same external situation. Your outside experience might be very different from the one you had as a child. However, the essence of the experience – your emotions and inner reactions to it – will be the same.

I've had many clients who've rehearsed a difficult conversation with me that they wanted to have with a child, parent or partner. As we've talked, they've communicated their viewpoint clearly, like kind, compassionate, eloquent adults. But as soon as they've returned home and actually tried to talk to the person in question, they've felt like an overwhelmed toddler with no idea of what to say.

When you try to have those kinds of conversations while you're in your emotional body, you'll find yourself becoming overdramatic, immature and single-minded. When you can resolve the emotional stress and speak from your heart and feeling body, though, you'll allow yourself to become the compassionate, kind, loving person you naturally are.

When that happens, you feel at one with the people you're communicating with and naturally begin to collaborate and co-create.

Sometimes, your emotional stress will have you so wound up that anything you try to say will come out sounding insane. In those situations, it can be incredibly helpful to have someone who'll just listen and allow you to rant as much as you need. If that person can patiently let the insanity run its course until you get to the other side, you'll probably find that you become aware of solutions as if by magic.

That said, it's important to realise that it can take practice to resolve emotional stress. Sometimes, no matter *how* much you might want to show up from your feeling body for your loved ones, you simply won't be able to in the moment.

We'll talk about this more in the next chapter, but for now, I want you to know that it's OK to ask for space. For example, you might want to say something like,

> "I'm feeling emotionally wobbly, but I'm not sure why. I love you, but I just need some space to sit with my emotions, tune in and see what they're saying."

And if someone else in your home is clearly experiencing emotional stress, you can lovingly offer them space in a similar way. (See Chapter 7 for more information on how to do this.)

## Effects on your home life

Of course, if unresolved emotional stress affects your ability to communicate, it's also going to affect your life at home.

That's because so much of what makes a home a warm, welcoming place to live is the daily flow of compassionate, loving, positive communication. It requires each person who lives there to show up as their best self – and to help each other show up that way too. And it requires each person to genuinely care about what's going on for everyone else and communicate that caring.

> Of course, if unresolved emotional stress affects your ability to communicate, it's also going to affect your life at home.

However, when you're experiencing emotional stress, you start to turn your focus inwards and forget everyone else. You can't even be *present* for other people, let alone show up the way you want to for them. Instead, you start blaming them for how you're emotionally feeling, and getting judgemental about their comments and actions.

We've already talked about how people in a home can take on each other's stress. The good news is that the reverse is often true as well. When you work on resolving your own emotional stress, the other people in your home will often transform too.

When this happens, you'll naturally start to see more synchronicity, joy, fun, happiness, peace and ability to receive. Rather than your home being a dumping ground of negative energy, you'll begin to connect with and share your wisdom with each other.

That means your home will become a haven in which your heart and higher self can sit down with you for a metaphorical 'cuppa'. Home might not always be perfect, but it will transform into a place where everyone living there feels safe to be exactly who they are.

## Effects on your intuition

You're naturally an amazingly intuitive person. I know this for a fact because *everyone* is.

Your intuition is available to you 24/7. It connects you with your heart and higher mind. It also connects you with the universe, God, angels, guides, your past loved ones, divine power and celestial beings.

It connects you with your past and future selves and with more than 8 billion other people on the planet, as well as animals, plants and all of nature.

You – *only always and in all ways* – have so much help and support available to you!

Unresolved emotional stress, however, can block this connection. It affects your ability to feel, trust and own your stuff. It shuts down your ability to discern your true feelings.

> Unresolved emotional stress can block your intuitive connection.

Additionally, sometimes you'll use unhelpful techniques to dull your emotional stress – for example, numbing out with TV, drinking or other addictions. These techniques also push down the voice of your intuition. Sometimes, they'll even make you forget you *have* a feeling body.

Your intuition can guide you through your emotional stress if you let it. And as you start to resolve the emotional stress, you'll feel your intuition begin to expand and activate.

## Effects on creativity

*"The creative mind is the source of your wishes, your desires and your aspirations.*

– Dr Bruce Lipton

Just as I can say with confidence that you're amazingly intuitive, I can also say that you're amazingly creative. Again, creativity is a natural state of everyone on this planet. And the free energy that we talked about in the physical health section also inspires our natural creativity.

We all love to craft and create, although that creativity takes different forms for each of us. There are *so* many ways we can each express our unique creative gifts. Mine takes the form of helping people to transform, understand and manage their emotional stress so that they live a life they love. Yours might involve sketching or painting. Your child's might involve building circuits with electronics sets or structures with blocks. One friend's might be cooking delicious food, while another's might involve sewing beautiful clothing.

Expressing those creative gifts and talents automatically creates the desire to share them. We long to contribute, both on a small scale to other people and on a larger scale to the planet. And we can *only always* identify ways to monetise those contributions to create abundant lives.

In fact, when we're in our naturally creative states, we can identify solutions – not just one solution, but many – for any problem, regardless of its size. So we can automatically see ways to not only enjoy our creative gifts but get paid well for them too.

> Just as with intuition, however, emotional stress affects our ability to express our creativity.

Just as with intuition, however, emotional stress affects our ability to express our creativity. It blocks our ability to see that a solution exists for every problem. It stops us from recognising our creative gifts and from accepting that we can monetise them. It stops us from remembering that emotionally connecting with ourselves automatically connects us with those we love via our hearts. And that connection is far more fulfilling than consumerism ever could be.

One of the best things you can do to help your children avoid developing emotional stress triggers around creativity is to repeatedly tell them something like,

> "Hey, that energy you're drawing with (or writing with or building those blocks with) is magical! If you spend your time doing things that feel good like that, your life will be wonderful, fulfilling and happy."

Resolving your emotional stress will unlock creative ideas and inspiration from within your heart and let them shine in your life and your home.

## Effects on your ability to function

In the section about how unresolved stress affects communication, I talked about reverting back to the age you were when a trigger first occurred. You'll find that triggers will keep occurring over and over throughout your life – apparently randomly. This is a process that I call emotional cycling.

Remember that the situation itself may not be anything like the one that first triggered you. However, the emotion it generates will be very familiar and will affect more than just your ability to communicate. It can also affect your ability to function as an adult.

> Emotional stress can affect your ability to function as an adult.

For example, if emotional stress makes you revert back to being, say, seven years old, you're going to find it very hard to take care of yourself. Things like being financially responsible, monetising your creativity or sometimes even just cooking your dinner will start to feel impossible.

In a more extreme example, I had one client whose emotional stress had kept him from ever forming real relationships with anyone other than his wife. He completely idolised her and felt as though it wasn't worth the effort of showing up emotionally for anyone else. After all, he got everything he thought he needed from her.

Once she died, however, he was left totally alone. So he not only had to deal with the grief of her passing. At the same time, he also had to start rebuilding all his other relationships from the ground up. AND, on top of that, he had to relearn how to take care of himself practically and do all the little things she used to do for him.

Perhaps your emotional stress makes you feel like someone else should be 'doing it all for you' and leaves you resentful if they don't. Or perhaps you just ignore self-care basics like eating healthy food, getting enough sleep or staying on top of housework and home admin.

Healing and managing your emotional stress makes it much easier to 'adult' in your daily life. It can also help you to reach out and create connections with other people that will turn into loving, rewarding relationships.

And that, in turn, makes your home a happier place and your life a smoother, more enjoyable experience.

## Effects on your spiritual intelligence

We started to talk about spiritual intelligence in Chapter 2. At that point, we defined it as the confidence that 'you have everything you need, exactly when you need it'.

> The *vibration* you put out is what you get back.

I want to expand on that definition now to incorporate the idea that the *vibration* you put out is what you get back. You might have heard this concept described as the Law of Attraction.

Regardless of what you call it, however, it's a fundamental idea that underpins spiritual intelligence. Why? Because if whatever's coming back to you is the *vibe* you've put out, it means you're automatically equipped to handle and manage it. It means you know with 100% certainty that you have everything you need exactly when you need it.

That, in turn, means you realise deep down that there's no such thing as a problem without a solution. You know at the deepest possible level that the universe has your back.

End of story – *only always*!

However, unresolved emotional stress makes you forget your natural spiritual intelligence. It makes you forget that there are always many solutions to a problem and that they're all available to you from within your heart and higher self.

Instead, you default to your conditioned belief systems where there *are* no solutions. You think you need to either put up with a problem or run away from it. In the back of your mind, you're hearing echoes and whispers of limiting beliefs like:

- 'I'm not good enough.'
- 'I'm just not up to scratch.'
- 'It's all too hard.'
- 'There's no time or money.'
- 'It's all been done before.'

If you're not hearing them about yourself, you're probably thinking them about people you love who are following their heart's and creative desires.

When you learn to manage and grow with your emotional stress, you'll remember that you *are* enough and you *do* have everything you need. We all have the same ability to tune into our hearts and connect with our higher selves.

You'll remember that a viable solution exists for every problem. And 100% of the time, the solution is right next to the problem. How quickly you solve it just depends on where you choose to focus: the problem or the solution.

## Effects on your ability to receive

Like everyone else on the planet, you're an energetic being. That means that not only can you contribute but you can also *receive* support. Your cells are like little solar panels that get their charge from the sunlight above them.

Instead of getting their charge from sunlight, however, your cells get it from the things you love doing and the people you choose to have in your life. And when they're fully charged, you feel free, empowered, abundant and able to deal with anything.

A tree shows you this: you never see it lifting its roots or running towards where the water or sunshine is. Instead, it just stays still and completely trusts that everything it needs will come to it. And you're just like that tree. You have the same ability to receive that it does.

> Emotional stress completely blocks your ability to receive.

However, emotional stress completely blocks your ability to receive. It puts a cover over your solar panels, blocking the incoming sunlight so you can no longer absorb it.

Here's how that might look in practice:

- You might have a partner who shows you a lot of love, but your emotional stress stops you seeing it or stops it from feeling real.
- You might refuse to get therapeutic help – for example, from a counsellor, massage therapist or even just from time in nature – when you need it.

- You might be extremely talented, but your emotional stress keeps you from receiving abundance and prosperity in return for your creative gifts.

- You might feel frustrated because you're the only person who cooks at home, and your emotional stress stops you accepting help from family members.

In each case, the problem isn't with your partner, the availability of the right therapeutic help, the economy *or* the cooking. It really isn't. Instead, the problem is with your ability to receive the energetic love, support and help that you long for and which is already *only always* there.

Managing your emotional stress will help you to identify what's really going on. It will also – if necessary – help you to ask for the assistance and support you desire.

## How to transform emotional stress into conscious clarity

Over the last few pages, we've talked about the many negative effects of unresolved emotional stress. But, as I mentioned earlier in the chapter, emotional stress is only negative if you ignore it and leave it unresolved.

So how do you start to transform your emotional stress into the conscious clarity that helps you to develop spiritual intelligence and emotional maturity? It all starts with self-awareness: you need to become aware of the specific beliefs that are relevant to the emotional stress you're experiencing.

Note: this isn't just about developing any old awareness. It needs to be an awareness that personally relates to you and your individual situation. When you develop that awareness, you'll *feel* the shift.

It will be undeniable.

And when you can shift your emotions, the situation will *only always* transform into something far better.

When that happens, you'll find yourself automatically opening up to new possibilities. You'll no longer need to defend your choices or argue with other people about theirs. You'll find the courage to have uncomfortable conversations, but you won't need to express anything other than your own truth.

And you'll be able to express that truth lovingly and easily.

## Start by paying attention to your emotions at home

Journaling about the questions in the exercise at the end of this chapter will help you to start to develop this awareness. However, the first step to understanding emotional stress is really to begin to become aware of your emotions at home.

> Remember that who you are at home is who you *are*.

Remember that who you are at home is who you *are*. So it makes sense that developing the emotional awareness you need to help you to heal emotional stress will start with paying attention at home.

Begin by asking yourself what your emotions are really saying about all the daily activities you carry out in your home.

When you ask this, I don't want you to think intellectually about how you feel. Nor do I want you to assume that you feel the emotions you think you 'should' feel. Instead, I want you to check in with your emotional body at regular intervals during the day. Start to pay attention to how it truly responds when, for example, you're:

- cooking
- doing laundry
- eating meals
- balancing your finances
- communicating
- making love.

I guarantee you that as you look at each of these activities through the lens of emotional awareness, you'll start to find places where emotional stress is hiding. Only once you do can you begin to resolve that stress… and all its consequences.

# Chapter 4 Exercises

**Exercise 1**

Out loud, ask yourself,

> "As a family or as an individual, what proportion of my communication is filled with the emotional drama of the day compared to the emotional happiness?"

Play with the question. Take the time to observe yourself in new ways.

**Exercise 2**

At home, really be the observer. Develop a deep understanding and awareness of what your emotional body is really doing (or has been doing) at home.

As you do this, start to explore what you're really feeling at home.

**Exercise 3**

Look back over the list of household activities on the previous page.

List them out, one per line, in your journal.

Then, one by one, go through the list and ask yourself how you really feel emotionally about each activity.

Write down the emotion you currently feel next to the activity in your journal.

If you feel a negative emotion (or just feel nothing) about any activity, pick a positive emotion that you'd like to feel instead. Again, you can choose one from the list in Appendix B.

Write this emotion next to the negative one.

Finally, for each activity, put your hand on your heart and say out loud,

> "Body, I choose to feel the emotion of [xxxx] when I'm doing [activity]."

## Chapter 4 Summary

1. Emotional stress, like an emotional wobble, is a sign that your thoughts and beliefs are out of alignment with your heart and higher self.

2. Emotional stress can show up at any time and can be passed from one person to another and from one generation to another.

3. Unresolved emotional stress can have significant negative effects on your health, intuition, creativity, home, communication, ability to function and more.

4. Transforming emotional stress into conscious clarity starts with self-awareness.

CHAPTER 5

# How to Manage Emotional Stress

## Resolving emotional stress takes more than just knowledge

In the previous chapter, you learnt quite a bit about emotional stress. You learnt where it comes from, how it can affect you and why it can be a good thing. At least, you learnt why it can be a good thing IF you resolve it.

However, it's not enough to simply know about emotional stress. You also need to take concrete actions to resolve and heal it. And the best specific actions to take will depend on three things:

- how intense the emotional stress is
- how long it's been building
- your own unique personality and preferences.

That's why, in this chapter, I'm going to introduce you to the concept of the emotional stress scale. It's a scale of emotional intensity that runs from 1 to 10. Level 1 reflects emotional stress that's subtle enough to feel like a gentle spring breeze, while Level 10 feels like a full-on Category 5 hurricane.

I'll help you to understand what exactly you need to do to heal and resolve stress at each level, and what help you might need. By the time you reach the end of the chapter, you'll have a much clearer idea of how to manage your emotional stress. You'll also understand how taking action when you're still somewhere low on the scale – even if nothing actually feels 'wrong' yet – can transform your entire life.

First, though, I want to introduce you to another client of mine, Mary (as always, not her real name). Here's what Mary's life looked like when she first came to see me…

## Mary's story: there's something about Mary…

As a mum in her forties with two young children, Mary was all too used to ignoring her own needs and emotions to focus on everyone else around her. In fact, when she first came to see me, she would have sworn that she didn't HAVE emotional stress. She would have said that she very rarely reacted emotionally to anything.

What was actually happening, however, was that she *did* have emotional wobbles – just like anyone else on the planet. She just completely ignored them. She subconsciously pushed them back down where they could turn into emotional stress. And without being expressed or acknowledged, that emotional stress had begun to create real physical effects in her body.

Mary didn't realise that, of course.

She just knew that both of her shoulders had frozen up and that she could barely lift or rotate either arm. She'd been to her doctor twice to get cortisone shots for pain relief. Both times, after a few weeks, the pain lessened a little.

As soon as it did, however, Mary was overwhelmed by a flood of intense Level 9 emotions that rushed to the surface. Not only that, but the pain also started shifting around her body. If she didn't feel it in her shoulders, it appeared in her diaphragm. And as soon as it lessened in both locations, her emotions started screaming at her to unpack them.

Soon, her fitness had begun to go downhill, and between the pain and intense emotions, she started turning into a hermit. Over time, she'd withdrawn from everyone and everything in her life, even to the point of considering moving interstate and leaving her husband.

She originally came to me for energy healing on her shoulders, but I could see that her symptoms were rooted in emotional stress. Mary was a very busy person – and I noticed she was subconsciously *staying* busy to avoid acknowledging how her triggers affected her.

Effectively, she was running away from them by burying herself in her work and family commitments. When that didn't work, she'd use alcohol. And when even *that* didn't work, she'd start to fantasise about leaving it all behind – teetering on the edge of moving states and leaving her family.

## Why use the emotional stress scale?

As you learnt in the previous chapter, everyone's emotional stress can look different. In turn, that means the most effective way to manage the stress can differ from person to person and situation to situation.

As a general rule, though, there are three broad categories of emotional stress intensity:

> The most effective way to manage emotional stress can differ from person to person and situation to situation.

- **Level 7–10**: at this level, the stress is intense and has probably been building for some time. It will almost certainly have reached a level you can no longer ignore. It will be generating some serious negative effects, not only in your life but in the lives of the people around you.

You'll probably have to make some fairly big changes in your life to manage and resolve any stress at this level.

- **Level 4–6**: at this level, the stress is either less intense, has been around for less time, or both. At this point, the effects it's creating might not be pleasant, but they're at a level that our culture tends to encourage us to ignore and push on.

However, unless you listen to Level 4–6 stress and deal with it, it will inevitably build up to a Level 7–10. And since it's far easier to deal with at this level, I strongly recommend taking steps to manage it now… *before* it can build.

- **Level 1–3**: stress at this level will be subtle – so subtle that you'll need to pay close attention to even notice it. In fact, as you'll discover later in the chapter, some of the signs of stress at this level won't actually FEEL like stress. They'll feel more like little taps on the shoulder or nudges from the universe.

In an ideal world, you'd notice stress at this level, then immediately stop and resolve it before it had a chance to build. However, we're all human, so it's important to know how to recognise and resolve stress at higher levels as well.

## Short-term discomfort creates long-term gain

As you read this chapter, your limiting beliefs and patterns will probably tell you all kinds of things about why dealing with your emotional stress isn't practical. They might tell you something like:

- you don't have time – maybe you're trying to meet a deadline
- you can always work on this emotional stuff later when you're less busy

- this symptom probably isn't related to emotional stress – maybe it's just a headache
- you're overreacting – surely you should be able to tough it out
- you'll drop the ball and fail to meet your responsibilities if you stop to deal with it.

Please know that none of these stories or excuses are true.

The truth is that there's NOTHING more important for you or the people around you than listening to what your emotional stress is saying and following its guidance.

I promise you that the long-term benefits – many of which you read about in the previous chapter – will more than outweigh any short-term discomfort this causes.

With that in mind, let's start by talking about the most intense levels of emotional stress.

> There's NOTHING more important for you or the people around you than listening to what your emotional stress is saying and following its guidance.

## Level 7–10 in emotional stress

### What it looks like

If you've allowed your stress to reach a Level 7–10, it's now at a point where it refuses to let you ignore it any longer.

On the next page are some of the signs and symptoms of stress at this level that you or the people around you may notice in you.

| Repetitive communication symptoms | Mental symptoms |
|---|---|
| • yelling or screaming<br>• throwing tantrums<br>• blaming other people.<br>**Action symptoms:**<br>• physically hurting yourself<br>• physically hurting someone or something else<br>• frequent pacing<br>• experiencing addiction<br>• crying uncontrollably<br>• throwing items. | • obsessive thoughts<br>• feeling as though you're losing your mind<br>• believing that nobody and nothing can help<br>• wanting to stay in bed for days (or even years!)<br>• longing to run away from everything and everyone<br>• thinking about killing yourself or wishing you were dead. |
| Health symptoms | Intense emotional symptoms |
| • any chronic pain or condition (eg. Mary's shifting pain)<br>• any serious illness, especially if it's not responding to physical medicine. | • self-pity<br>• jealousy<br>• rejection<br>• confusion<br>• overwhelm<br>• insecurities. |

## What to do at a Level 7–10: soothe the stress, then get help

When your emotional stress reaches this intense level, it's like you're standing at the bottom of a mountain that you know you need to climb.

You know the summit is somewhere up there, but you can't see it, and you can barely even see the bottom of the broken path that leads up the mountainside. All you can really see are the immediate obstacles around you.

Stress at this level interferes with your ability to see what's truly going on around you and blocks your ability to make good decisions. For example, in Mary's case, it told her that the smart decision was to leave her family behind and just run away.

Trying to come up with a workable plan to make changes in your life while your stress is peaking just won't work. So before you can do anything else, you need to stop, briefly step back from daily life and soothe the stress.

> When your emotional stress reaches this intense level, it's like you're standing at the bottom of a mountain that you know you need to climb.

### Create a 'Self-soothing Actions' list

The best way to soothe stress differs for everyone, and it can be hard, in the moment, to identify what self-soothing actions will work best for you.

That's why I recommend creating your own personalised self-soothing actions list during a time you're not actively in the grip of an emotional wobble. Write your favourite self-soothing actions on it and keep this personalised list handy – perhaps on your fridge and/or on your phone. Then, the next time you start to feel your stress peaking, refer back to it for actions you can take.

On the next page, you'll find a few recommendations for soothing actions that often work for my clients.

| At home indoors | Outside your home |
|---|---|
| - take a bath<br>- let yourself sleep or nap<br>- connect with your pet<br>- cook or eat nourishing food<br>- cry and release the stress through tears<br>- talk it out – perhaps with a soft toy<br>- organise something in your house<br>- scream in private. | - take a 'mental health day' off from work, university or school<br>- walk along the beach<br>- get out into nature<br>- give your time to someone else<br>- scream in your car<br>- do some kind of vigorous exercise. |
| **At home outdoors** | **Anywhere** |
| - stand barefoot on the grass<br>- get outside and feel the sunshine<br>- work in your garden. | - listen to music that suits your mood<br>- dance it out<br>- sing alone or to music<br>- write it out. |

## Using your 'Self-soothing Actions' list

When you realise that you're in the grip of emotional stress, the first step is to set an intention to soothe your stress. This will also activate your heart and higher self to 'drop in' an awareness of what will heal the stress internally.

You'll probably notice yourself wanting to think about the trigger – the external situation or event you think 'made' you feel emotionally stressed. You might also be tempted to focus all your attention on blaming or fixing that trigger. You might really want to vent to a friend or family member and project your stress onto them. Or you might feel tempted to keep ignoring your stress altogether and denying that it's even a problem.

DON'T.

Don't do any of these things.

Instead, remind yourself that you're *only always* responsible for your own emotional reactions. There might well be something that your heart and higher self want to guide you to change about the way you act or show up. Right now, though, you're not in any state to hear that guidance clearly.

> Remind yourself that you're *only always* responsible for your own emotional reactions.

To get yourself to that point, you *must* soothe your emotional stress. Ask your body to guide you to the action on your list that will best help to soothe you. Perhaps you could say something like,

> "I'm feeling emotional stress, and I know I need to soothe it out. What will best do that, body?"

Then pick the one action on your list that feels as though it will be most helpful for you, and DO it in that moment.

Remember: before you even consider talking to someone else you care about and taking your stress into their space, you need to soothe it.

## How NOT to manage your Level 7–10 stress

Our culture offers us a wide variety of examples of unhelpful ways to 'soothe' and 'manage' our emotional stress.

Which of the following have you noticed in yourself?

- yelling at people you love
- hurting or abusing someone else
- getting sick regularly
- repeatedly complaining about the same thing, eg. a physical problem
- playing the victim and refusing to accept you have the power to change anything
- always escaping into work and a never-ending to-do list
- using alcohol or drugs – either recreational or prescription – to escape
- constantly blaming or gossiping about your spouse, child or friend
- regularly experiencing problems with money and finances
- experiencing strong emotional outbursts and storms
- living in clutter and mess.

It can be very tempting to fall back into these patterns and behaviours when you're feeling intense emotional stress.

But I want to be very clear that this is NOT OK.

It's not OK to 'talk something out' with someone you care about while you're in the grip of strong, uncontrollable emotional stress. It's not OK to discuss things when you're intoxicated, or in a fit of rage, blame or depression.

In fact, if I have one rule about emotional soothing, it's this:

> *Do NOT take your emotional stress out on other people in your home, no matter what!*

Do NOT take your emotional stress out on other people in your home, no matter what!

If you notice that you've slipped into this intense emotional state, take yourself away from other people. Let them move away from you if you know you're showing up this way.

Take responsibility for soothing yourself, using the techniques you learnt earlier in this section. Then take responsibility for reaching out to a professional for help.

Only once you've done these two things should you consider talking to the people you care about as part of managing and healing your Level 7–10 stress.

### Once you've self-soothed, get outside help

In almost every case I've seen – both personally and professionally over the past two decades – ongoing, repeated Level 7–10 emotional stress needs professional outside help.

I can't overstate the importance and value of getting a professional to help you internally unpack and resolve your stress.

Friends and family are often just too close to the situation to help you see it clearly the way an outsider can. They're also very rarely trained to give you the guidance and space you need.

If you notice yourself regularly having to self-soothe emotional stress at this level, it's a definite sign that you need outside help. Ignoring your Level 7–10 stress isn't an option. You learnt how dangerous it can be for your health and wellbeing in the previous chapter.

Trying to deal with it completely on your own can be almost as dangerous.

### Imagine your emotional stress as a broken bone

If you'd broken your arm, you wouldn't try to set it yourself, or ask an untrained friend or family member to fix it for you at home, right?

> If you'd broken your arm, you wouldn't try to set it yourself.

Instead, you'd go to a professional, get it x-rayed, set properly and then put into a cast so that it could heal. Perhaps the doctor you saw would also prescribe an appropriate painkiller. And then, once the cast came off, they'd prescribe a set of exercises to strengthen your arm muscles and restore you to full function.

You might even end up better off than you were before you broke your arm.

If you tried to manage the broken bone at home, it wouldn't (hopefully!) be long before someone who cared about you said, "Oh no! You've broken your arm, and it's clearly causing you a lot of pain. Let's get you to the doctor NOW so you can get it x-rayed!"

Imagine if you let your ego stop you getting that x-ray. Imagine saying, "Nah, I don't need a doctor. It's not really that bad, and it'll heal fine on its own if I just ignore it."

The pain would continue, likely getting worse and worse over time. The bones would probably heal at a bad angle – creating even more long-term problems. You might never regain the full use of your arm.

So of course you'd head to the doctor and get professional help for that broken bone.

In the same way, the right therapist (or team of therapists) can help you heal your emotional stress and restore you to full function. They can help you to transform your emotional stress into conscious clarity that leaves you in a better, more functional place than you were to start with.

## What to look for when you seek professional help

For any professional help to work, you'll need a therapist who's confident they can:

- once and for all resolve your Level 7–10 emotional stress internally
- help you communicate about your Level 4–6 emotional stress to stop it building up to Level 7–10 stress in the future.

This therapist could work in any number of modalities, and some might work in more than one. Their specific modality doesn't matter. What matters is that they expect to create results for you – and that you expect to get those results and to do what it takes to achieve them.

When you actually reach out, try to connect from a place of empowerment, rather than one of negativity.

For example, try to avoid thinking:

- "Something's very wrong with me if I need help."
- "It's too much money to get myself help."
- "One day, I'll stop doing this."

Instead, make a conscious decision to think something like, "I'm going to talk to a great therapist about this and get some more tools to help me work this out in my home. Then I can show up in the best possible way for everyone in my home."

With the right professional help, you can not only resolve all your Level 7–10 emotional stress but also become aware of less intense

> With the right professional help, you can not only resolve all your Level 7–10 emotional stress but also become aware of less intense stress when it happens.

stress when it happens. That means you'll eventually develop the tools to recognise and manage stress at a Level 1–3 long before it causes serious problems.

### Additional outside help

As well as (not instead of) getting professional help, I recommend educating and upskilling yourself by regularly:

- taking workshops about self-awareness/conscious communication
- listening to podcasts and reading self-help books on the subject
- watching Gaia TV regularly
- finding a hobby or creative activity you love and consistently take time to do it
- taking a holiday, either away or at home.

These are all realistic, actionable steps that will help you to heal and resolve intense stress faster than you'd imagined possible.

## Level 4–6 in emotional stress

### What it looks like

The next category down from Level 7–10 emotional stress is Level 4–6. At this level, you'll usually know that something's not right, but you may have simply become used to ignoring it.

Interestingly, signs that you're at Level 4–6 in emotional stress don't always show up within you. They can also show up in your environment and in the way in which the world interacts with you. Often, they'll directly mirror externally whatever's happening on the inside.

Remember in the Introduction how Sarah ended up with a drawer that wouldn't open? She'd been working with me for long enough that she realised it was a clear message about her own 'stuckness'.

That's why you'll notice that the final group of symptoms below are all things that show up in the outside world. So if your emotional stress is in this range, you and the people around you may notice some of the following signs.

| Health symptoms | Lifestyle symptoms |
|---|---|
| • headaches or body aches<br>• restless sleep<br>• colds and sniffles<br>• cuts, bruises or stubbed toes<br>• nail-biting. | • feeling constantly busy, but not getting much done<br>• often rushing and/or rushing others<br>• regularly feeling distracted with a busy mind. |
| **Reactive behaviour symptoms** | **Outside world symptoms** |
| • criticising, complaining, being picky, or never being satisfied<br>• sulking, getting defensive or speaking harshly<br>• being pessimistic or just giving up<br>• acting from insecurity, over-pleasing or attention-seeking. | • losing your keys<br>• getting stuck in traffic<br>• the internet going down<br>• burning your cooking<br>• a sudden drop in customers or business<br>• clutter around your home. |

Note: the reactive behaviours I've mentioned above are some of the most common. However, there are many, many other types of reactive behaviour, so you'll find a more comprehensive list in Appendix C.

## What to do at a Level 4–6: soothe, get feedback and change the culture

When your emotional stress is at a level in this range, it's as though you're halfway up that mountain we talked about earlier. You can see much more than you could at the bottom… but your journey isn't over yet.

> When your emotional stress is at a level in this range, it's as though you're halfway up that mountain we talked about earlier.

The self-soothing techniques we talked about in the Level 7–10 section can also help with emotional stress in this range. So if you feel the need for soothing, that's your first step.

Then, once you've soothed your stress, you may be able to ask other people in your home for their feedback, rather than needing a professional. That's especially true if the other people in your home have done the same work as you to develop emotional maturity and manage their own emotional stress.

If you can't talk to the people in your home, however, find someone else. It might be someone you're close to from your childhood family or a good friend. Choose someone you completely trust and who you know won't judge you.

### How to ask for feedback

Once you know who you'll speak to, say something like the following to them,

> "Hey, I can feel a lot of emotional stress in my body. I'm emotionally wobbly and it's overwhelming me. Can I talk to you to help me understand what's going on? I just really want to talk out what's happening with me presently."

Or say,

> "Hey, I can feel some emotional stress presently. I'd like you to just listen to me and encourage me to find my own answers. And if you see something that I don't seem to be aware of, can you just ask me whether you can share it with me? I may want to continue exploring and find it myself, so if I say no, please support that."

That word 'presently' is really important. It helps you to stay in the present moment where everything actually happens.

Just as important is letting the person you talk to know that you don't want them to fix the situation for you. You just want to talk it through until you've reached a point where you can become aware of what's going on for yourself. Then, when you're finished, you might be open to their feedback

Alternatively, if you know – or think you know – exactly what's stressing you out, you could approach the conversation a little differently. Think back to a possible example we mentioned briefly in the previous chapter – the one about feeling resentful because you're 'always the person who cooks'.

Instead of stewing in that resentment, you could ask for help and feedback to connect with what's really going on for you. Perhaps you could say something like,

> "I've been thinking about cooking at home. I imagine it looking one way, but I'm seeing it happening completely differently. What does your imagination say about it?"

Or,

> "I'm confused about being the only person who cooks dinner in our home. Could you please help me understand why I'm the only one cooking?"

Or,

"I'm becoming resentful about being the only one who cooks dinner, and I don't like showing up this way. I don't mind cooking, but I want my passion and joy for it back. Could you help me understand what could be wobbling me? Why am I making this about cooking when I know I love to cook for our family? I'm not getting it."

Remember that 'cooking' is just an example here. It could be anything: cooking, organising, communicating or cleaning. What's important is that it's something you realise has become a trigger for you for no apparent reason.

Talk authentically about what you're feeling and experiencing, focusing on that rather than on the external trigger. Or, if you do talk about the trigger, speak from the perspective of using it as an outside sign that there's something internal to be aware of.

### *Remember that emotional stress makes you regress in age*

As we discussed in Chapter 4, when you're under emotional stress, you revert to the same age you were when you first encountered the trigger for that stress.

Imagine that you're 33 now, but when you're emotionally stressed, you regress to being 3 years old again. All the parts of your emotional brain that developed after you were three start to shut down. That means you're limited to communicating the way you did back when you were three.

And that's why you can start seeing yourself throwing tantrums or sulking – you've psychologically regressed to the age where that's just how you communicated.

So next time you find yourself throwing a tantrum or sulking, speak out loud to your body. Say something like,

> "Hang on, how old am I right now? Body, come back to my present age and consciousness."

Then say,

> "Body, how can I love and support myself right now? Do I need to give myself some space, or would I like to talk it out with someone else?"

This will help you to realign with the current moment and your current age. Only once you've done that will you be able to consciously make effective choices.

And then, hours later, you'll be able to reflect on what happened from a place of clarity. You'll see what you could have done differently… and you can grow and do better next time.

*This requires changing the culture in your home*

To manage your Level 4–6 stress, you'll need to start learning some basic communication and self-awareness techniques. It will feel awkward to open up and authentically share at first, but I encourage you to stick with it until the techniques flow smoothly and easily.

Start by only acknowledging how you're feeling within yourself, using something like the dialogue scripts above. Then, as your home culture becomes one of authentic, judgement-free sharing, you can also start to acknowledge what you're seeing in other people too. For example, you might say something like,

> "Hey, I can sense/feel that you've got some emotional stress going on. Do you feel like talking it out with me or someone else? I'm happy to listen, and I believe you've got this. If I feel

I have something to offer, I'll ask you before I share it, but it's safe for you to open up and find your own answers."

Do your best to develop a culture in your home where this kind of sharing is seen as inspiring, accepting and supportive. And then, if you're the one listening, do just that. Don't offer your own opinions without asking whether it's OK – and if the answer is 'no', then respect that.

Remember: it's not about you being right. It's about the other person connecting with their heart and higher self. This will help them to become aware of the possibilities that are available to them.

This new culture will help to create a vibe of warmth, safety, connection and growth.

And that, as we've already discussed, is the foundation of an emotionally happy home.

## Level 1–3 in emotional stress

### What it looks like

If your stress is at a level in the 1–3 range, it's subtle enough that you may not even realise it's there. That means you'll need to proactively pay attention and look for it to benefit from its wisdom.

In some cases, you might feel a mild emotional wobble – perhaps a momentary flash of irritation, a whisper of frustration or the slightest hint of a headache behind one eye. Other subtle feelings and signs might include:

- feeling vague, 'not with it' or daydream-y
- wanting to eat or drink more or less than usual
- continually forgetting things
- making a lot of little mistakes.

In other cases, the universe will send you an external sign via a subtle intuitive nudge that there's something to pay attention to. It does this to help you stop and connect to your heart and higher self, which will help you to easily and lightly become aware of possible messages. Examples might include:

- nature, colour or number symbols that have meaning for you (for example, noticing '11:11' when you look at the time)
- seeing apparently random movement out of the corner of your eye
- apparently random words from a book, TV show, movie or sign that feel meaningful.

And sometimes, you'll simply feel your intuition gently nudging you to do something to raise your vibration like:

- stopping to look at something
- picking a spiritual card
- putting a crystal in your bra or pocket
- watering your plants
- calling your mum, dad or grandparents
- eating that salad
- practising some yoga.

When you move into these spaces and raise your vibration, look for awareness that drops in from your heart and higher mind. It's *only always* there.

## What to do at a Level 1–3: pay attention, listen and be guided

> When your emotional stress is in the Level 1–3 range, you're almost at the top of the mountain.

When your emotional stress is in the Level 1–3 range, you're almost at the top of the mountain. You can see all around you, with a clear view that stretches out in all directions. There's just a little bit further to go to get to the summit. With a little effort and clear intention, you can tune into your feeling body and access direction and great wisdom.

At this stress level, your body will probably first try to tell you to pay attention to something using the gentle, intuitive nudge I mentioned above. It doesn't always happen this way – everything is case-by-case – but starting subtle is the most common progression.

Ideally, at this point, you'll notice the nudge and say something like:

- "Yeah, I can feel something."
- "I can sense something."
- "Oh! What's that?"

Unfortunately, if you're like most people, you've been conditioned to ignore subtle signs. So you'll probably either dismiss what you notice or immediately blame it on something external. You might say something like:

- "Oh, it's nothing. I just need to get on with things."
- "I don't have time to look at this. I'll do it later."

- "I must have just slept badly last night."
- "It's because I stared at my computer screen for too long today."

Then, if your body's initial nudges don't work, you're likely to start getting those external nudges from the universe. And if neither of *those* work, your body will probably have no choice but to create a mild emotional wobble to get your attention.

## Never ignore Level 1–3 emotional stress

No matter how tempting and more convenient it may be to ignore the nudges and minor wobbles of emotional stress at a Level 1–3, DON'T.

If you can pay attention and do some self-enquiry at this level, your life will flow *so much* more smoothly. You can also make your self-enquiry fun and light, instead of heavy and hard.

Start by asking your body to share its wisdom. Say something like,

> "OK, body. I'm sensing something. Feeling body, have you got direction for me?"

Listen to the answer. Stay present and tune into your heart and higher mind, the way I did in the shower in the case study in Chapter 4. If a feeling comes up, listen to it and follow it wisely. Or, if nothing comes, say,

> "Come on, body. Let's just take 10–20 minutes to internally review."

Then, before you do anything else, set the intention to discover what your emotions are sharing with you. Ask your heart and higher self to talk to you.

In the next chapter, we'll talk about an emotional hygiene technique I call the 'emotional shower'. This technique can be very helpful to provide insight into Level 1–3 emotional stress.

You can also use practices such as:

- sitting somewhere quiet and journaling about how you're feeling
- relaxing by meditating, having a bath, listening to music or doing yoga
- using any of my systems that you've learnt outside of this book or any other systems you love – self-muscle testing, in particular, can help to fast-track your exploration.

Finally, once you discover the source of the emotional stress, it's time to look for a solution. If you can't immediately sense one, ask your heart. Placing your hand on your heart centre while talking out loud to your body magnifies your ability to hear what your heart and higher self are saying.

Start by saying out loud,

> "OK, I'm sensing that I have emotional stress. I know there's a solution to it. What do I need to become aware of?"

What if you have a stubborn mind that continues to say, "There's no solution, nothing to be aware of and no way forward"? In that case, put your hand on your heart again, then ask,

> "If there *was* a solution, what would it be?"

Again, trust that your heart and higher mind will come through for you and just listen for the awareness. It WILL come.

## Mary's story: there's something about Mary, continued...

Curious about how Mary's story ended once she started to work on her stress?

Well, as Mary and I worked together, she realised that any emotional wobbles under a Level 9–10 on the emotional stress scale just didn't register for her. She'd become so good at pushing them down that, as far as her conscious mind was concerned, they simply didn't exist.

So we started helping her by getting her to use some of the techniques you've learnt in this chapter to first soothe, then heal and resolve her Level 7–10 stress. Once it no longer blocked her ability to accept help, she began to work with an osteopath and massage therapist. This helped with her external symptoms, while she and I together addressed the internal causes.

We discovered that Mary had a lot of internal stories telling her that nobody cared what she thought or how she felt. Once she started to acknowledge and heal those stories, she began to recognise just how much support she had available from her husband, family and wider circle.

Then, we worked on helping her to recognise stress at Level 4–6. That way, she could deal with it in the moment, instead of allowing it to build up. And, finally, I started teaching her how to pay attention when subtle wobbles and external signs of Level 1–3 stress showed up.

Today, Mary's life looks very different. She lives an emotionally happy, abundant life where she feels surrounded by love. She recognises just how much support she has available to her from her husband and kids. When an emotional wobble turns up, she acknowledges it, talks it through with someone she trusts, learns from it and allows its wisdom to guide her.

Her shoulders have never frozen up again since then.

## Chapter 5 Exercises

**Exercise 1**

Next time you're feeling emotionally stressed, self-analyse where you are on the scale by asking your body out loud,

> "Body, where am I on the emotional stress scale? Am I at Level 1–3? Am I at Level 4–6 or even Level 7–10?"

Your body will instantly connect to your higher mind and heart, and let you know.

Then take appropriate action.

**Exercise 2**

When you're at any emotional stress level, but especially Level 7–10, notice the 'emotion' you get stuck in the most. DON'T focus on the outside experience or situation that's triggering you. Instead, focus on the emotion.

Perhaps your most common emotion might be impatience, frustration, fear, anxiety, failure, shame, resentment, depression or instability?

Once you can name this emotion, remind yourself that ALL emotions are a choice. Ask yourself what you wish to feel instead.

Perhaps it's satisfaction, confidence, calmness, success, acceptance, happiness or stability?

If you're not sure, refer to the list of positive-feeling emotions in Appendix B. Then, try to transform your emotional state in the moment. If you don't know how to, ask your body. For example, you might say something like,

> "Body, I notice that I'm feeling frustration. Please find a way to transform this into satisfaction."

Know that your higher self and heart will action this. Then try to become aware of what they tell you and act on it.

Practise this until you can nail it.

Once you do, you'll be able to transform ALL your higher level stress into Level 1–3. It will fall away like a leaf on a tree. Remember that Level 7–10 stress will also need outside professional help.

## Chapter 5 Summary

1. It's useful to categorise levels of stress on a scale of intensity that runs from 1 to 10.

2. If you're at Level 7–10, soothe your immediate stress and then get professional help to transform it into conscious clarity.

3. If you're at Level 4–6, seek feedback from someone you trust and connect with to help you understand it.

4. If you're at Level 1–3, STOP and take 10–20 minutes to look within and connect with what your heart and higher self are saying.

5. Realise that Level 1–3 emotional stress is subtle and can show up as external nudges. Don't ignore these nudges when you notice them!

CHAPTER 6

# Personal Emotional Hygiene

## Emotional hygiene: the art of proactive emotional stress management

Over the last couple of chapters, we've talked about the dangers of built-up emotional stress and how to heal it.

In itself, however, resolving that emotional stress isn't enough to create an emotionally happy home. Yes, it will probably make *everything* at home feel dramatically better... for a while. But unless your habits change going forward, the emotional stress will eventually just start to build again.

It's like when you do a deep clean and declutter after not doing any housework for years. Everything looks so beautifully shiny and spotless straight afterwards... but unless you start making a habit of proactively keeping things clean, the clutter quickly builds back up again.

> The most effective way to manage emotional stress can differ from person to person and situation to situation.

Then, eventually, you just end up right back where you started.

That's why, in this chapter, we'll be talking about emotional hygiene: the art of proactively managing your stress *daily*.

However, the emotional hygiene practices you'll learn in this chapter will do more than just help you to avoid building up toxic levels of emotional stress again. Once you start practising these techniques every single day, they'll open up a world of magic where:

- your heart and higher self are suddenly available 24/7 for infallible guidance
- your creativity blossoms and you discover your own path to fulfilling contribution
- you discover with delight that the universe really does *only always* have your back and that everything you need is provided exactly when you need it.

Plus, when you practise emotional hygiene regularly, you'll find it far easier to make good decisions about looking after yourself physically. That means you'll automatically gravitate towards eating better, going to bed earlier, moving your body more often and hydrating well. Consistently making great choices will stop feeling like such a struggle.

To give you an idea of the difference that ongoing emotional hygiene can make in your life, let me introduce you to another client, Darren (of course, not his real name).

## Darren's story: starting with the man in the mirror

Darren was a repeat client who was now in his 50s. Back when we'd first worked together ten years ago, he'd had great success with my techniques. At the time, he'd needed to deal with some deep-seated emotional stress before he could fully step into his business. And once he'd resolved that stress, the results had been dramatic.

His business had skyrocketed, growing rapidly into a multimillion-dollar entity. In the decade since I'd last seen him, life had become everything he'd dreamed of. He had a gorgeous house, a flashy car, and he and his wife Jenny regularly took expensive holidays all over the world.

He loved working and focusing on his business, while Jenny, who had a quieter nature, relished her role as a homemaker and mother to their two children. But once their kids grew up and left home, everything seemed to change. By the time he was ready to retire, he realised with dismay that home just wasn't a place he enjoyed being any more.

Without their kids to focus on, his loving wife seemed to have transformed into someone else. Jenny constantly snapped at him, preferring to spend her time with her head down buried in the Facebook feed on her phone rather than talking with him.

On top of that, they were having serious problems with Jenny's mother. His mother-in-law was a bitter woman who'd had a string of failed relationships and now did her best to ensure that he and Jenny were equally unhappy. Darren knew exactly how they needed to compassionately manage Jenny's mother, but any time he tried to share his wisdom, Jenny snippily shut him down.

When he looked around at all his friends, he saw they were getting divorced. He couldn't help wondering if that was the logical answer for him too. But some part of him knew that he loved Jenny, and he didn't want to give up on their relationship without a fight.

So, remembering the results of our earlier work, he booked another appointment with me. He wanted to ask whether there was anything he could get Jenny to do that would fix things. It seemed obvious to him that the problem lay with her. After all, *she* was the one who'd completely changed. *She* was the one with such poor emotional hygiene that she couldn't even talk to him now without biting his head off.

Or was she?

When we started using muscle testing to talk to Darren's emotional body, a very different story emerged. He didn't want to believe it, but the clear message he received was that, actually, the problem was about him and HIS emotional hygiene.

As we worked together, he realised that he'd focused so intently on his business over the past decade that everything else – including his emotional hygiene – came a far distant second. He'd effectively left Jenny alone to manage everything on the home front, unaware of all the changes she'd experienced as their kids grew older and her primary role in life transformed.

He'd never had to practise any emotional hygiene to contribute to the culture of connection and communication in their home. Jenny had always done all that. And while she'd had the kids to focus on, that hadn't been a problem. Now, however, she felt empty and unfulfilled. And a home with only the two of them in it shone a harsh spotlight on Darren's own poor emotional hygiene.

Unless he started with 'the man in the mirror', his emotional body told him, their relationship would never recover.

## Emotional hygiene is much like physical hygiene

Imagine you've just got back from a ten-day hiking trip along a muddy, forested mountain trail.

Without the convenience of running hot water, your daily shower probably fell by the wayside. Perhaps you replaced it with a cursory swipe of a pre-moistened wipe most days or a quick dunk in an icy stream whenever one was available. But I bet it wasn't the thorough shower you're used to taking each day. If you had to boil all your drinking water, you probably brushed your teeth less often too. And you almost certainly didn't do regular laundry or wash your hair on your usual schedule while you hiked.

Regardless, by the time you get back to civilisation, you're probably feeling pretty gross. There's only so much a pre-moistened wipe can do, so chances are that you're smelling fairly ripe. Your mouth probably feels like something's growing in it, and your clothes are likely to be smeared with mud and dirt, and smelling kind of rank as well.

So the first thing you do is dump your clothes in the washing machine. The second is take a long hot shower, thoroughly wash your hair, brush your teeth and then put on clean clothes.

Only after all of *that* do you hug your kids, climb into bed with your partner or spend time in close proximity with anyone else you care about. After all, you don't want to inflict all that dirt and stench on anyone else when it's so easy to clean it up, right?

That's also why, when you're *not* out hiking muddy trails, you stay on top of your physical hygiene. You just don't ever let yourself go days at a time without a shower. You automatically brush your teeth twice a day. And you put clothes you've worn next to your skin aside for laundry as soon as you take them off.

It's just a matter of basic consideration.

## Emotional hygiene is just as important

Unless you practise regular emotional hygiene techniques – the emotional equivalents of taking a shower and doing your laundry – you'll start to emotionally stink. That's even truer if any of the people you love are highly sensitive.

> Unless you practise regular emotional hygiene techniques – the emotional equivalents of taking a shower and doing your laundry – you'll start to emotionally stink.

In other words, practising emotional hygiene isn't just about avoiding the kind of emotional stress build-up we talked about in Chapters 4 and 5. It's also about acting with basic consideration towards the other people in your home and life.

Those aren't the only similarities between emotional and physical hygiene either. Others include:

- **Avoiding serious problems:** failing to practise physical hygiene – especially around washing your hands regularly, for example – can also lead to serious disease. And we've already talked about how failing to practise emotional hygiene leads to the bigger emotional stress issues.

- **Growing old well:** looking after and nurturing your physical body by practising physical hygiene – amongst other things – leads to it looking after you. The result is that you age well. Similarly, looking after and nurturing your emotional body by practising emotional hygiene results in it looking after you as you age. You'll have fewer accidents, illnesses and age-related degeneration.

- **Getting clearer on what works for you:** when you keep yourself clean and healthy physically, it's much quicker and easier to identify things that don't work for you. You rapidly discover what scents you like, what fabrics feel good on your skin and what foods make you feel energised. Similarly, when you keep yourself emotionally clean, it's much easier to recognise what makes you feel good and bad in the moment.

And, with practice, you can make emotional hygiene techniques *just* as much of an automatic habit as your daily showers, tooth-brushing and laundry.

## So what exactly is emotional hygiene?

Earlier in the chapter, I described emotional hygiene as the art of proactive emotional stress management. It's a catchy description… but what does it mean in practice?

At its heart, emotional hygiene is about proactively taking 10–20 minutes to check in with yourself and figure out what's actually going on emotionally for you. It's about understanding and becoming aware of what's happening in your life and how what's happening makes you feel emotionally. It's also about connecting with your heart and higher self to identify whether or not you need to take any action in response.

> At its heart, emotional hygiene is about proactively taking 10–20 minutes to check in with yourself and figure out what's actually going on emotionally for you.

To help with this, you might try spending 10–20 minutes on any one of the following techniques:

- journaling about what's bothering you or going on around you
- meditating
- walking, sitting or playing in nature
- taking a power nap or rest
- sitting quietly with a cup of tea
- listening to music
- playing an instrument
- practising a few yoga asanas
- colouring a mandala
- gardening
- exercising of some sort
- having a physical shower/bath.

One of the best structures for these techniques is taking an emotional shower, which we'll talk about later in the chapter. For the meantime, though, I just want you to think of emotional hygiene as – exactly like a physical shower – something you need to do everything single day.

## Incorporating pleasure and play

Another aspect of emotional hygiene is taking time for – and prioritising – things that genuinely give you pleasure. Your emotional body loves to play and have fun, and allowing it to raises your vibration.

So in addition to 'standard' emotional hygiene techniques, don't forget to *regularly* incorporate fun and pleasure into your life. Create a list for yourself of ten or so vibration-raising activities that you enjoy and that you'd happily do for hours if you could.

Some of these activities might be the same as the ones that soothe you, while others might be different. Some of the most common include:

- enjoying a long, hot, scented bath
- picking flowers from your garden
- creating a garden to pick flowers from
- doing a jigsaw puzzle
- reading (either fiction or non-fiction – whichever you enjoy most)
- watching a favourite Netflix or Gaia series
- listening to music
- watching or playing sport
- decorating or renovating your home
- doing something creative: perhaps cooking, art, pottery, drawing or building something
- drawing oracle cards
- journaling or other creative writing
- researching an upcoming trip
- decluttering an area or room of your house.

## Good emotional hygiene needs to happen daily

A few hundred years ago in our Western culture, nobody would have believed it was possible for an average person to devote half an hour every single day to bathing.

That's partly due to technology – without indoor plumbing and a hot water system, drawing a bath took a long time and a lot of effort. So unless you were rich enough to afford servants, or had the time and money to visit a public bathhouse, there just weren't enough hours in the day. Soap also had to be handmade, so it was a rare and expensive commodity. As a result, bathing as we know it happened far more rarely.

And because the link between hygiene and disease hadn't yet been discovered, average people saw no reason to pay daily attention to keeping clean.

Today, of course, those of us living in Western countries usually have easy, relatively cheap access to hot running water. So for most of us, hygiene is just a matter of turning on a tap and using an inexpensive bar of soap picked up at the local store.

We also understand the link between cleanliness and health. So, as a result, we prioritise a daily bath or shower as an accepted – and expected – part of our lives. And if someone chooses not to bathe regularly, we regard it (and sometimes them) as a genuine problem.

> Emotional hygiene practices should take no more than 10–20 minutes per day.

I want you to start thinking of emotional hygiene in exactly the same way. On the surface, emotional hygiene practices might look as though they demand a lot of time. The truth, however, is that most days, they'll take you no more than 10–20 minutes.

And yes, it's true that many people today still don't understand the link between good emotional hygiene and emotional health. You, on the other hand, have already learnt a great deal about *why* emotional hygiene is so important. You already know enough to make it every bit as much of a priority as physical hygiene is.

Now you just need to learn specific techniques to make it a quick, simple, automatic daily practice.

## Darren's story: starting with the man in the mirror, continued...

As Darren and I started working together again, he realised he'd been making a LOT of assumptions about what Jenny wanted. Most of them, he discovered, were based on spending money on her. After all, that's all he'd been contributing to the relationship up until that point.

So, for example, when she'd said she needed a break, he'd booked an expensive, luxury vacation, flying business class and staying in the finest five-star hotels. Or when they went out somewhere together and she admired a flower, he'd go home and buy her a huge bouquet of three dozen red roses.

As he started practising his emotional hygiene more regularly, however, he realised that what Jenny really wanted was for him to be present with her. He discovered with shock that she buried herself in her phone when he was near because she found him genuinely unpleasant to be around. She thought he was always in his head and that he showed up as sulky, angry and uninspiring.

No wonder she'd felt uncomfortable! And she'd been trying to tell him that she was unhappy, but he hadn't been able to hear her. Instead, he'd just thrown money at the issue and expected that to fix it.

Together, Darren and I started rewriting some of his limiting beliefs about his ability to communicate and contribute in non-financial ways. We addressed some of his childhood triggers and insecurities, and slowly but surely, his beliefs in the present changed… and so did his actions.

Instead of getting irritable and 'humph-ing' when he saw Jenny on her phone, he'd get playful. With a twinkle in his voice, he'd say, "Wow, I wish I were that phone right now!" If she admired a flower as they were out walking, he'd make a mental note of it, and then later, sneak back and pick it for her.

And like magic, his relationship with Jenny transformed. It's now stronger than it's ever been – and she's even started to seek out his wisdom about dealing with her mother. His relationships with his kids have transformed too – even though he's done nothing actively to work on those.

Now, Darren is continuing to see me once a month – and not because anything's wrong now. Instead, it's because he loves the feeling of constantly learning and discovering more about himself.

## It starts with changing your beliefs

*"Beliefs and thoughts alter cells in your body."*

– Dr Bruce Lipton

The first place to start when you're practising emotional hygiene is with your belief system. You already believe that a daily shower or bath is easy to fit into your schedule, right? You probably also believe it's easy for everyone else in your family to do too.

So now you need to update your beliefs around daily emotional hygiene to match those you have for physical hygiene. For example, you might choose a new belief that goes something like,

> "I believe I can stop and explore my emotions and thoughts whenever I choose."

Or,

> "I believe it's easy to stop and manage my emotional stress."

Or,

> "I believe it's soothing to care for and nurture my emotional hygiene every day."

Or,

> "I believe others support me taking an emotional shower whenever I choose."

Or,

> "I believe it's pleasurable to explore my emotions."

Or,

> "I believe it's valuable to understand what my emotions are saying to me."

Or,

> "I believe I *only always*, and in all ways, give myself whatever I need to manage, understand and care for my emotional wellbeing."

The next thing you need to realise is that you have around 50 trillion cells in your body. Imagine they're like a movement – a force of people who are ready and willing to do whatever you instruct them to do. You could imagine them as a network of 50 trillion devoted social media followers. Each one is ready to pass on your message to their own networks and do whatever they can to make your wishes happen.

When Darren wanted to figure out what was going on in his communication with Jenny, he harnessed his 50 trillion cells by speaking to them directly. He literally said, "Body, help me to understand what Jenny really wants. Help me to listen to her emotions and not her words." And then he paid attention to the awareness and messages his body immediately responded with and acted on them.

Can you imagine how powerful the force within YOUR 50 trillion cells could be if you harnessed it?

Use your cells to help you bring your new belief into reality. To encode it, go outside and put your hand on your heart. Stand on the grass (if possible) with bare feet, then walk around and say the new belief out loud 5 to 15 times until you 'feel' it.

> Can you imagine how powerful the force within YOUR 50 trillion cells could be if you harnessed it?

At this point, it will feel easy to say, and you'll notice an undeniable feeling dropping in to your body. This gets the belief out of your head, and as all 50 trillion of your cells take it on, you'll embody it, not just intellectually speak it.

Keep working with the belief until you undeniably feel it embodied within you. Then watch as your external reality begins to reflect it.

Then commit to living as if your new belief were already true. Look for and notice examples in your life of times when it turns out to be true.

## You CAN transform your beliefs

As you consider this new belief, you'll probably hear some kind of inner voice telling you that you 'can't' believe it, because it's not true. Maybe that voice will say, "I can't practise emotional hygiene daily because…," followed by any one of a zillion excuses.

> All your stories are based on your existing beliefs and past conditionings.

Remember that it's just a story your mind is telling you, and all your stories are based on your existing beliefs and past conditionings.

Any time you want to venture out of your comfort zone, it's your mind's job to keep you safe by coming up with all the reasons you shouldn't. That's all that's happening here.

The important thing is to recognise that your current negative limiting beliefs *are* a choice. You may not have consciously chosen to take them on originally. Maybe you absorbed them from your childhood family or formed them early in life in response to events that happened to you as a child.

But that doesn't mean you're stuck with them.

I know it sounds confronting, but however your beliefs originally formed, you can change them NOW. If you don't like what your beliefs are creating, you get to choose new ones.

And once you genuinely believe that you can, it's time to start incorporating emotional showers into your life.

## How to take an emotional shower

> *"We are what we repeatedly do. Excellence, then, is not an act, but a habit."*
>
> – Aristotle

OK, you've updated your beliefs to reflect that not only is it possible to practise daily emotional hygiene but it's also desirable and even pleasurable.

So what do you do next?

The go-to technique I recommend using daily is the emotional shower. As I mentioned earlier, you can take an emotional shower in just 10–20 minutes, which means it's something you *only always* have time for. Then, once you've 'stepped out of the shower', you'll have a much clearer view of what's really going on for you and what you need to do about it.

Here's a quick, easy step-by-step guide to taking an emotional shower

### Intention setting: getting undressed

**Before you do anything else for your emotional shower, talk to your body out loud and say something like,**

> "OK, body. What am I sensing? What are my emotions saying right now? Is there anything on my mind currently? Is there a potential change on the horizon? If so, how do I imagine it happening? And what do I need to believe to allow it to happen with ease?"

This allows you to access your heart and higher self through your 50 trillion cells. It creates a portal for your intuition, awareness and insight to come through.

And if you start to feel something, but you're not sure what it is, ask your body to clarify its message. Say something like,

> "I really want to understand what you're trying to show me, body. I can sense something. Please communicate it to me more clearly."

Once your intention feels solid, let yourself expect your body to guide you easily towards the answers you're looking for. In the same way that you'd simply *expect* to come out of a physical shower feeling fresh and clean, let yourself feel the same level of expectation around your emotional shower.

Then, when you can really sense that expectation, you can actually step into your emotional shower.

## Showering: getting clean

On the surface, taking an emotional shower is simply taking 10–20 minutes out to practise one of the emotional hygiene techniques we talked about earlier in the chapter.

However, it's your initial intention – and the questions you follow up with – that set an emotional shower apart from more general emotional hygiene.

So pick an activity and do it. This will raise your vibration, which will then make it easy for your heart and higher self to step in. That's all there is to this part ☺.

## Follow up: towelling off and getting dressed again

Once you've finished with the shower proper, it's time to ask yourself three questions. You'll probably find it useful to pull out your journal and write down both the questions and your answers within it.

Here's what you need to ask yourself:

1. **What's my present story?**

   How are you really feeling emotionally right now, and what was the trigger that generated that feeling? Perhaps you're feeling angry with yourself because you're trying to eat more healthily and you had a junk food binge.

   In Darren's case, one of his stories was, "I'm frustrated because I can't communicate with Jenny. She never listens to anything I say, and everything I do say ends up being wrong!"

2. **What story would I like to shift this to?**

   With the clarity and awareness you've gained from your emotional shower, ask yourself what you'd prefer to believe instead. In the case above, you might tell yourself, "I almost always eat good food, but I don't need to be perfect, and I easily forgive myself when I slip up."

   In Darren's case, he set the belief that 'My intuition always guides me with inspiring things to say to Jenny. She loves the way I communicate with her, and she's started to automatically put her phone down when I walk into the room'.

3. **What emotion do I choose to feel instead?**

   How could you feel if you truly believed the new story you created in Step 2?

What might it feel like if, as in our example, you did believe that you almost always ate nourishing food and that you forgave yourself easily any time you didn't? The answer could be anything here: relieved, happy, relaxed, self-loving – the possibilities are endless.

In Darren's case, he was very clear that the emotion he chose was feeling nurtured – but yours could be anything you want.

See Appendix B for a list of options you might choose.

Once you finish writing your answers, I guarantee that you'll feel refreshed, clear and far more aware of what actions – if any – you need to take going forward.

## Chapter 6 Exercises

**Exercise 1**

This exercise will help you to uncover whether you have unconscious negative limiting beliefs that stop you from prioritising your emotional hygiene.

To do the exercise, say each statement below out loud, then tune into your body while listening to your thoughts. You might want to do this straight after you take your emotional shower, so that you're as clear as possible about any emotional responses you experience and anything you become aware of.

Here are the statements to say:

> "I'm going to give myself a couple of hours of downtime this morning."

> "I'm going to spend the morning with my loved one. Spending time together always makes me feel warmth and fun."

> "I'm going to sit in nature and journal about what's bothering me."

> "I'm going to see a great therapist and deal with this situation I'm in. I'm excited to discover which choices I'm making to create this reality and which new choices I can make to change it."

> "I'm going to take a day to myself and enjoy my creativity. Everything else can wait."

> "I'm going to take some time out to play in nature and recharge."

Then take out your journal and write down any stories that come up and how you feel emotionally about them.

**Exercise 2**

This exercise will help you to create your list of top ten activities for pleasure, play and vibration-raising, so that you can start incorporating more of them into your life.

1. What makes you smile and laugh out loud at home? What are the things that make you emotionally giggly? (I love this question!)

2. What do you do for yourself at home for pleasure, play and relaxation? How do you enjoy yourself at home?

3. From the list above and your memory of past experiences you loved that made you feel emotionally happy, create your list of top ten vibration-raising activities.

   Put this list on the fridge, in your office or somewhere you can easily see it.

## Chapter 6 Summary

1. Emotional hygiene deserves the same priority that you give to physical hygiene.

2. As with physical hygiene, you need to practise emotional hygiene at least daily.

3. Emotional showers are the foundation of emotional hygiene and take no more than 10–20 minutes each day.

4. An emotional shower starts with setting an intention and recruiting the 50 trillion cells in your body to help you find clarity.

5. Once you've taken your emotional shower, you'll feel refreshed, clear and clean – much as you would after a physical shower.

## CHAPTER 7

# Emotional Hygiene for Other People's Emotional Stress

## An emotionally happy home is about more than just you alone

I've said several times in this book that everyone's responsible for their own emotions and emotional hygiene. I stand by that assertion 100%.

However, all of us are human. We all make mistakes sometimes. We have bad days. We respond reactively to an emotional wobble. We say or do things we wish we hadn't (just think about my light switch story back in Chapter 1). And because who we are at home is who we are at the deepest possible level, those reactive, emotionally wobbly responses tend to happen predominantly when we're at home.

> All of us are human. We all make mistakes sometimes. We have bad days.

When you have this kind of messy, reactive response, one of the most comforting feelings in the world is knowing that the people you love have your back. They support you. They don't judge or criticise you… but at the same time, they don't allow you to continue treating them or yourself badly either.

This is what an emotionally happy home culture is at its heart. It's a culture where you can 'mess up' and still feel safe and loved by the other people in your home. In return, when someone else in your home 'messes up' or simply feels wobbly about something, you can extend the same love and safety to them. You can give them what they need – whether that's space, support or both – to find their own answers.

However, showing up in this kind of compassionate, loving way is easier said than done. When someone else is emotionally stressed and expressing it through reactive behaviour, it feels natural to get reactive in response.

That's why this chapter is all about how to practise emotional hygiene around other people's stress. As you work your way through it, you'll learn specific skills, techniques and scripts for communicating with someone who's emotionally stressed.

In many ways, this chapter is the culmination of everything you've read so far. These skills are the ones that will help you to create the culture of an emotionally happy home.

> *"All it takes is one person in any generation to heal a family's limiting beliefs."*
>
> – Gregg Braden

## Anne & Daniel's story: ever-expanding ripples of healing

When Daniel and Anne came to see me, they were desperate. Their family of five was on the verge of tearing apart.

First, there was Anne, who was on heavy medication to control her emotional outbursts. As Daniel commented, things weren't perfect with the medication, but they were far, far better than without. Of the three children, one was extremely defiant – constantly arguing and throwing tantrums when she couldn't get her way. The second, like his mother, was heavily medicated. In his case, however, the medication was for ADHD (attention deficit hyperactivity disorder).

Anne came to see me first. Within one session, I could see that she was highly sensitive to *everything* in her environment. It was like she was wearing a helmet that dialled up the intensity of every sound, scent, touch, visual cue and emotional inflection from everyone around her. She felt like everything in her environment was constantly yelling at her, demanding her attention.

No wonder then that she turned to prescription drugs to dampen the intensity of all that incoming sensation and emotional information.

However, high sensitivity wasn't all Anne had going on. She also had a LOT of emotional stress to unpack – some relating to her past and some to her present life. And because I knew that emotional stress doesn't happen in a vacuum, I asked her if Daniel would be willing to work with me too.

He was, and he told me that he was at his wit's end. He felt terrified that he'd end up losing his defiant daughter to any of the many life traps that can catch angry teenagers. If that happened, he was sure Anne would end up killing herself. He was willing for me to try anything with her... but he begged me not to take her off her medication.

Daniel knew the medication wasn't solving anything in the long term, but he was half-scared that Anne might kill him if she stopped taking her meds.

Now, while it's true that Anne had a lot of work to do, Daniel needed to realise that so did he. I helped him to see that his view of Anne as fundamentally 'broken' was creating a vicious cycle that only intensified her problems. And on top of that, he wasn't taking responsibility for his own emotions – his fears, insecurities and jealousy. He was putting the blame for everything squarely on her.

Once he started working on his own stuff, he cleared a space in which Anne felt safe to begin healing hers. And the positive results rippled out not only to the two of them but also to their kids and even their wider family members…

## All reactive behaviours are a cry for help

Back in Chapter 5, I briefly introduced you to the concept of reactive behaviours as signs of emotional stress. As a reminder, you'll find a comprehensive list of reactive behaviours in Appendix C, but some of the most common ones for Level 4–6 emotional stress are:

- criticising, complaining, being picky, or never being satisfied
- sulking, getting defensive or speaking harshly
- being pessimistic or just giving up
- acting from insecurity, over-pleasing or attention-seeking.

Then, for more intense Level 7–10 emotional stress, common reactive behaviours include:

- yelling at, hurting or abusing people you love
- constantly blaming or gossiping about your spouse, child or friend
- getting sick regularly
- escaping into work and a never-ending to-do list

- playing the victim and refusing to accept you have the power to change anything
- using alcohol or drugs – either recreational or prescription – for escape
- regularly experiencing problems with money and finances
- experiencing strong emotional outbursts and storms
- living in a cluttered mess.

What I want you to now understand when anyone around you acts in these ways is that you're seeing a clear desperate cry for help.

> When anyone around you behaves reactively, you're seeing a clear desperate cry for help.

This cry happens when the person concerned isn't aware of what's happening within them. They certainly aren't in control of it. They're feeling something they don't know how to manage. They're disconnected from their emotional body, and their behaviour is a way of trying to cover up that discomfort.

If you could translate the cry for help from their emotional body into everyday language, it might sound something like,

> "Please help me! I'm stuck! My heart and higher self are telling me to go one way, but my conditioned limiting beliefs are getting in my way. I need to create new, more empowering beliefs and programs, but I'm scared to feel the discomfort that requires!"

In our case study, Anne was showing several of these behaviours. She had frequent emotional storms, yelled at and abused the people she loved, and used prescription drugs to escape.

And while Daniel probably on some level recognised her behaviours as a cry for help and longed to 'fix' the situation, he had no idea of what to do. His sense of powerlessness – along with his own triggers – led him to his own reactive behaviours: blaming, criticising, feeling insecure and pessimistic, and playing the victim.

Until he learnt to unpack his own reactions, he couldn't create the space Anne needed to find her answers.

That's not to say that reactive behaviours don't, or shouldn't, have consequences. Sometimes the most loving thing you can do for someone who's behaving reactively is to set boundaries that make it clear that their behaviour isn't OK.

However, it takes skill and practice to set those boundaries from a calm, centred place of compassion. To do *that*, you need to first ensure that you're not behaving reactively yourself in response.

## How you treat other people is how you treat yourself

Unfortunately, most of us aren't any better off than Daniel when we're around people who are behaving reactively. What we're witnessing can feel unpleasant at best and like a personal attack at worst.

That's because we've all been conditioned from a very early age to believe that if someone's uncomfortable emotionally, it means something's really wrong. Not only that, but if someone's blaming us for their discomfort, it means there's something wrong with US.

So our standard response to other people's reactive behaviours is usually to try to 'fight or flee' by:

- figuratively 'running away' from the reactive behaviour – perhaps by deliberately ignoring it or using something (eg. drugs, alcohol or food) to dull its sting

- 'fighting back' against the behaviour – arguing with the person, defending ourselves if they're blaming us or counter-attacking with a long list of *their* faults.

The first thing that can really help when someone around you behaves reactively is to remember that however you treat other people is how deep down you treat yourself. By extension, that means that however someone's currently treating you is how deep down they're treating themselves.

> However someone's currently treating you is how deep down they're treating themselves.

This was a key insight for Daniel. When he finally *got* that the way Anne was treating him on the surface was the same way she was treating herself deep down, he burst into tears. How, he asked me, could this beautiful, vibrant woman he'd fallen in love with treat herself so horribly?

Realising what was truly going on inside Anne was a turning point for him. It released a wellspring of compassion from his feeling body, which in turn began to blunt some of the sting of her outbursts.

I guarantee that if you can see other people's reactive behaviour from this perspective, you'll be able to access the same wellspring of compassion within yourself.

## Everybody wants to grow and open to the light

The next step that can help when someone around you behaves reactively is to remember that nobody WANTS to act that way. There's not a single person on this planet who, deep down in their heart and higher self, wants to:

- feel out of control with their emotions
- yell, scream or say hurtful things to the people they care about
- stay stuck in limited, outdated beliefs and programs

- speak hatefully, resentfully or angrily
- treat others poorly or be treated poorly.

*Every* one of us wants to grow and open towards the light. And I do mean everyone. Even the 'worst of the worst' of us – the narcissists, psychopaths and sociopaths – want to reconnect with the light deep down in their hearts. They may not consciously know that they want this, but I promise you, the longing is buried deep in there somewhere.

So if it's true for the 'worst of the worst' of us, how much truer is it for the people in your life, who – hopefully – aren't any of these things?

## You can CHOOSE how you respond to reactive behaviours

I want to be very clear here that nothing I said in the previous section implies that you have to simply put up with reactive behaviour. We'll talk about the essential art of setting and communicating healthy boundaries later in this chapter.

For now, I want you to understand that you *only always* have a choice about how you respond to someone else's reactive behaviours. Realising that the behaviour is neither personal nor what that person truly wants can make it far easier to choose to respond with emotional maturity and spiritual intelligence.

It's easier, in other words, to respond with compassion.

The first step is actively naming what you're seeing in the other person from the perspective of your heart and higher self. You might say out loud or write in your journal something like,

> "OK, Steve's obviously emotionally stressed right now. His reactive behaviour is a cry for help. He doesn't want to hurt me or upset me. In fact, nothing in this is about me, and I can choose *my* response to it."

Or,

"Wow, Jessica's acting weird. She's all over the place. I know this is reactive behaviour and that it means she's crying for help. She must be stuck somewhere that feels really horrible on the inside. How can I contribute here?"

Or,

"I need to remember that how Tony's treating me right now is how he internally treats himself. He *wants* to grow. Everyone does. He wants to open to the light. This reactive behaviour means he needs some help. What can I contribute right now?"

The specific wording isn't important. The key is that you see this person you love behaving so reactively, then frame it to yourself as some variation of,

"What I'm seeing means they *really* need some help right now. Can I contribute anything or is it best to give them space?"

As you ask this, remind yourself that 'contributing' *isn't* about doing anything to fix the situation for them. In fact, trying to fix it is probably one of the least helpful responses you can have.

> 'Contributing' *isn't* about doing anything to fix the situation for them.

That's because, just like you, the person who's behaving reactively has everything they need to solve their issues when they need it. They just need to figure out how. So your contribution will never be about giving them the answers. Instead, it will be about providing them with the space to figure it out on their own.

That might mean offering a safe, non-judgemental ear so they can talk it out until they reach their own conclusion. Or it might mean giving them space to work through their emotional wobble alone until they're ready to talk it out.

Either way, you need to centre and ground yourself in a place of compassion and belief in their ability to find their answers. Once you can do this, your intuition will guide you as to how best to contribute.

And only *then* are you ready to communicate with the other person and offer your support.

## Your self-talk is as important as what you say out loud

It might be hard to accept initially, but your thoughts carry a lot of energy. So even if you don't speak any negative thoughts you have aloud, they'll influence the people around you. This is especially true of the people in your family and childhood family.

Even on a mundane level, your thoughts shape how you see other people. This, in turn, shapes your body language and the way you act around them. So allowing your negative thoughts to run unchecked will create separation above and beyond their energetic payload.

That's why you *must* keep a close eye on your thoughts when other people behave reactively. And regardless of what's going on externally, don't allow yourself to think things like:

- "He just doesn't want to find a solution."
- "They never listen, so what's the point?"
- "My thoughts make zero difference to anyone."
- "They're absolutely hopeless."
- "She's never going to change."

Instead of focusing your thoughts on the reactive behaviour, focus on what you'd love to see from the other person.

A few thoughts you could try replacing the ones above with might include:

- "He's got this! I know his heart and higher self are guiding him."
- "They can hear and understand me; deep down, they respect what I believe."
- "I know my thoughts *only always* create and influence my reality."
- "It is working out for them. Their heart and higher self are already aware of everything they need."
- "It's exciting to watch her easily change, grow and evolve."

Stay emotionally strong and solid with these new, positive thoughts. Keep repeating them over and over in your mind until they become natural beliefs about everyone in your family and childhood family.

Remember: you're capable of helping yourself. So is everyone else in your home.

## Don't ignore your history with your childhood family

As you're exploring your thoughts about the person who's behaving reactively, keep an attentive eye out for any thoughts that feel familiar.

Back in Chapter 4, we talked about how emotional triggers form early in your life. Then, as you experience situations that make you feel the way the original triggering situation did, you'll feel the same emotions again.

This repeating pattern is also true of the thoughts and beliefs that formed around your original triggering situation. So, for example, let's say you notice a negative thought about your partner that 'he never listens to me!' Then, when you look back at your early life, you might realise you created *exactly* the same story about your father after a triggering situation.

> Because we spend so much of our early years close to – and influenced by – childhood family members, they're one of the most common sources of our original triggers.

In these circumstances, you'll almost always need to work on healing and resolving the original story before you can truly rewire your current beliefs about your partner.

Because we spend so much of our early years close to – and influenced by – childhood family members, they're one of the most common sources of our original triggers. That's why I encourage everyone who's working on emotional hygiene to explore their primary thoughts about each member of their childhood family.

I've included an exercise at the end of this chapter to help you do this.

## How to communicate about reactive behaviours

Communication really is the key to an emotionally happy home. But it has to be candid, compassionate communication. The communication that creates an emotionally happy home is gentle. It's kind. It's clear. It's patient. It's honest. It has integrity.

And most of all, it's not done to only make the communicator feel better emotionally.

In this section, I'll give you some specific scripts for communicating with other people in your home about their reactive behaviours. However, if you know that clear, emotionally mature communication is a weak point for you generally, I encourage you to work on this as a priority. You could try:

- doing a communication course
- reading books on the subject
- watching documentaries or TEDx talks
- working with a therapist who's trained in spiritually intelligent and emotionally mature communication skills.

Upping your communication game will help you with EVERY area of your life. It will be particularly helpful for 'difficult conversations' about reactive behaviour, though.

With all of that in mind, once you've communicated with *yourself* about the other person's reactive behaviour, it's time to communicate with them.

If you're like many people who've grown up in our culture, this idea might make you nervous. And I want to acknowledge that, sometimes, talking with someone about reactive behaviour might make you genuinely fear for your physical safety. In those cases, it's important to not only give the reactive person space but also to get professional one-to-one help to work through your individual situation.

In most cases, however, physical violence *isn't* what we're scared of. Instead, we're nervous about the discomfort a conversation will create. We're scared of saying or doing the wrong thing and making the problem worse. Or we're frustrated because we feel like we should be able to fix the situation.

> There's nothing to be scared of when you're communicating with someone you love about their reactive behaviour.

And in all those situations, I want you to know that there's NOTHING to be scared of.

That's important enough that I'm going to say it again: there's nothing to be scared of when you're communicating with someone you love about their reactive behaviour.

Remind yourself that it's OK to feel uncomfortable. It's just an emotional wobble – one you can work on yourself, on your own, without making it part of the communication. Remind yourself too that nobody's expecting you to fix anything.

Then, finally, remind yourself that you don't need to worry about saying or doing the wrong thing. All you're going to do is ask what the other person wants.

Then, when you're ready, say something like,

> "Hey, I can see you're emotionally stressed right now.
> Would you like to talk about what's going on,
> or would you prefer some space?"

After that, just listen and give them whichever option they ask for.

### If they want to talk it out, be there for them

To your ego, this can feel like the 'best' option for a reactive person to choose. In truth, however, it's no more or less valid a choice than asking for space would be. And the key to making it work is as simple – and difficult – as listening.

That's it. Listen, listen, listen.

Use your whole body and all your senses. Watch their body. Watch what they're doing. Listen to their words and their tone. It will all help you to understand not just them but yourself as well.

Keep in mind that your ONLY job as a listener is to give the other person space to talk about what's currently inside them.

> Your ONLY job as a listener is to give the other person space to talk about what's currently inside them.

You don't need to solve anything.

You don't even need to *say* anything except to let them know you're hearing them, that they'll find their own answers, and that you're there for them until they do. And perhaps, when they seem to have talked themselves out, you can ask them if they want to say anything else.

As they talk it out, you might use words like,

"Yes, I can understand you. What you're saying is valid. I get it."

Or perhaps say,

"Thanks for trusting me enough to share. Would you like to tell me more?"

If they come to a conclusion that seems flawed to you, don't try to 'fix' it or convince them that they're wrong. Instead, say something like,

"You know what? If that seems like it's going to work for you, try it and see."

The whole time, as you're listening, come from the perspective of seeing them as someone who really does 'have this'. You can express this out loud if it feels right to – perhaps by saying,

"You've got all the answers inside you. Trust yourself. I'm here to listen. I love you. Everything's OK. Things will *only always* work out for you."

Remember: they already have everything they need.

They just need to become aware of that.

## *What if you don't WANT to listen?*

While it's natural to feel nervous about this kind of communication initially, the conversation shouldn't feel heavy as it happens. It should feel exciting to help your loved one discover more about themselves and to play a part in them uncovering new solutions and growth.

However, sometimes that's not the reality you experience. You might feel a sense of dread or frustration during the conversation. That can be especially true if it seems like you've had the same conversation multiple times and nothing ever changes afterwards.

If you're *not* enjoying the sharing, try to keep listening while the other person is talking. Remember that the discomfort you're feeling isn't about what the other person is saying. It's about something that's coming from inside you.

Then, later on, at a time when you *can* make the conversation about you, I encourage you to say something like,

> "Babe, can you help me, please? I'm struggling with my thoughts and focus when you talk to me about [topic]. My thoughts are negative, and I find that I just want to move away and not listen to you. It sounds to me like you're covering the same thing over and over again.
>
> I love you and us, so I don't want to feel this way. Can you let me know what's really going on for you?"

Then, again, listen to what they say and let your intuition help you choose how best to respond.

## If they ask for space, give it to them

If the other person says they want space, believe them and let them know you respect their choice. You might respond with something like,

> "No worries, I'll be around. If you want to talk about it at any point, I'm happy to listen and let you hear yourself. In the meantime, I know you've got this. See you later."

> If the other person says they want space, believe them and let them know you respect their choice.

The key is to trust them to know what they need. Don't badger them to talk or insist on trying to fix the situation for them.

Instead, physically move away from them. As you do, affirm to yourself that whatever it is they're dealing with, they've got it. Their heart and higher self will help them to sort it out, just as yours would (and does) for you.

Then find something to do that will help you to stay in that mindset while they work through the situation on their own.

## If they keep being reactive, set boundaries

Sometimes, no matter how emotionally mature your communication is, the other person is simply too stressed to hear you. Perhaps they respond by:

- trying to make it all about you
- continuing to blame someone or something else
- refusing to take responsibility for anything about the situation

- believing it's impossible to change or transform for whatever reason
- being prickly, sarcastic or just unpleasant to be around.

When this happens, the best thing you can do for them and yourself is to physically move away from them – just as you would if they'd asked for space.

Remind yourself that they've got this. If you need to, say it out loud – perhaps something like,

> "I know they've got this. I know they can and *will* help themselves. Everything's OK. Things always work out for them."

Any other thought pattern only enables their fears, doubts and insecurities.

Remind yourself too that this kind of emotional maturity takes a lot of practice. It's OK not to get it perfect the first few (or the first many) times, as long as you don't give up.

However, if you find it intensely challenging – so much so that it's hard to even try – I strongly recommend getting help. Reach out to a professional who's skilled at guiding clients through emotionally mature communication.

Because until you master this ability, you'll never have a truly emotionally happy home.

Finally, once you've done this, set your boundary. Let the person know that you want to be there for them, but that you can't be there for their behaviour. For example, you might say,

> "Hey, babe. I can see right now that you're feeling real emotional stress. Is there anything I can do to help? I'm happy to listen to what's going on or give you space if that's what you need. I'm not happy to be your punching bag, however."

Or you could say,

"Babe, the way you're showing up with me right now is how you show up to yourself. So if I keep letting you treat me this way, I'm telling you it's OK to treat yourself that way.

I love you way too much to do that, so while you're doing it, I'm just going to step back and give myself some space.

Everything's OK. I'm not walking out on you, but I am walking out on this behaviour. It's getting us nowhere, and it's hurting us both. When you're ready to connect or know what's really going on, let's talk about it."

Then physically walk away to maintain your boundary. You might go into the next room or out for a walk. In an extreme situation, you might even decide to sleep in another room for a few nights until the reactive person is ready to take responsibility for their behaviour.

At a later point, if they have taken their stress out on you before you could set a boundary to prevent it, you might say something like,

"Babe, I'd like to talk about the other day when [be more specific here if you need to]. I don't feel comfortable or safe in our home when you take your stress out on me and show up that way. I'd like to see a change here."

## Communicating with emotionally stressed kids

In the scripts above, I've assumed that you're communicating with another adult – perhaps your partner, a relative or flatmate. Either way, you're talking with someone who has the same level of life experience and capacity to take responsibility for themselves that you have.

However, when the emotionally stressed person is younger, the scripts need to change a little. They need to include more age-appropriate language.

> When the emotionally stressed person is younger, the scripts need to change a little.

For example, for an older child, you might say,

> "Hey, honey. How you're treating mum right now isn't how she wants to be treated, so I'm going to give you some space.
>
> I'm here to talk if you need me. Other than that, I trust you to understand for yourself what's going on for you. And then, when you're ready and willing, I really want to learn about what you need so I can help you understand yourself."

Perhaps you might also add,

> "If I've done something that you feel has contributed to how you're feeling and behaving, could you please let me know. I want to know and understand your side."

Or if your child is younger, you'll want to keep it simpler. Perhaps physically get down on the floor with them, then say something like,

> "Honey, I can see that you're really stressed now. What can Mum or Dad do to help? Is there anything we can help you with?"

If they're not verbal yet and can't speak back, you could say the above words without expecting a reply. Then, once you've said the words, hold a calm energy and do something to distract your child.

## Watch out for your stories...

As you think about communicating with someone about their reactive behaviours, you'll probably notice a sense of resistance coming up. If you explore this resistance, chances are that you'll discover that it's based in stories like:

- "I should just let it go."
- "I can't rock the boat."

- 🦋 "Everything's OK now, so I should just ignore it."
- 🦋 "Talking about it won't work."
- 🦋 "Nothing will make this better."
- 🦋 "What if they get angry again?"
- 🦋 "What if we don't talk or have sex for a while?"
- 🦋 "What if they leave me?"
- 🦋 "They're too young to understand."

> As you think about communicating with someone about their reactive behaviours, you'll probably notice a sense of resistance coming up.

**DON'T listen to these stories.**

They're all about you, and what you stand to gain or lose from a conversation. They're not about the person you love, and the growth and healing that person might access from working through their stress.

Remind yourself of how much you love them, and then communicate clearly and calmly.

It's just a conversation.

It's OK to feel uncomfortable.

The discomfort is absolutely worth it to find a real resolution – and for that person, and your relationship with them, to evolve.

*"Spirituality must be lived not just studied. All the books in the world will not help us if we do not live what we learn."*

– Kryon

## Anne & Daniel's story: ever-expanding ripples of healing, continued...

For Daniel, it was a huge step to go from seeing Anne as somehow broken and incapable to seeing her as someone who'd really 'got this'. But he couldn't do any of the other work he needed to do until he'd mastered that.

Then, as he and I worked together, he learnt how to set emotional boundaries around Anne's harsh behaviour when she spun out. He learnt to let her know that he wanted to be there for her, but that he couldn't be there for that behaviour.

He also learnt how to simply listen to her, and that if something she said triggered something in him, it was up to him to unpack it at a different time.

For example, one of their major relationship stressors was that Anne was no longer interested in being sexual with him. She hadn't stopped noticing men altogether, however. Anne herself felt immensely guilty about this, and Daniel felt as though his jealousy would rip him apart whenever she paid any attention to other men.

Once, far back, Anne had started to talk about her feelings and Daniel had been furious. He'd felt so jealous and stressed that he'd literally wet their bed that night – and then he'd made the mishap 100% Anne's fault.

One of the hardest lessons for Daniel to learn was that if he loved Anne, he needed to let her talk freely about what was really happening inside her. Then, if her comments triggered something in him, it was up to him to unpack that at another time.

As she finally talked her feelings through, Anne became very clear that she never wanted to cheat. She just wanted to honestly acknowledge what she felt. She also realised that a great deal of her sexuality-related stress was rooted in a deep shame she felt about an episode of innocent childhood sexual exploration.

And as she worked through and healed this stress, she discovered she was 100% ready to talk to her doctor about coming off her medication.

Interestingly, as Anne and Daniel's relationship began to strengthen, evolve and deepen, so did the other relationships in their home.

Their defiant daughter, who'd constantly thrown tantrums and threatened to vandalise her classroom, changed enough that her school noticed. They were so impressed, in fact, that they invited me to give a presentation to the teachers on how to handle similar students.

The son who'd needed such high doses of medication for his ADHD was able to come completely off his medication too.

But the ripples didn't stop there. Anne discovered that she wasn't the first person in her childhood family to feel such deep shame about innocent childhood exploration. The topic came up with her father, and it turned out that he'd had a similar experience as a child. Being able to talk his experience through with Anne freed him from its chains.

Daniel too had a sister who was an alcoholic. By learning to change the way he thought and talked about her, he opened up a space in which she could begin to heal. And that's exactly what she did, to everyone in his family's amazement.

Today, Daniel and Anne's relationship is rock solid. She channels her sensitivity and passion into a career in music, while he enjoys a range of creative pursuits.

Best of all, nobody's on drugs and nobody's defiant or spinning out.

## Setting up your home culture for success

The techniques you've learnt in this chapter have the potential to be useful in any situation where someone's behaving reactively. However, they'll be most powerful in a home where everyone already understands the concepts of emotional hygiene and is willing to take responsibility for their own stuff.

They'll also be more powerful in a home where everyone knows they're safe – and that they'll be supported – if they're honest about what they need. A home where they know that asking to talk through something won't result in someone swooping in to try to fix it for them. A home where they know that asking for space won't hurt anyone's feelings or make anyone believe the problem is their fault.

Because of this, I recommend getting everyone in your home to read this book – yes, even your kids if they're old enough. Then, once you're confident that everyone understands the basic concepts, talk about them – ideally during a time when everyone is receptive and nobody's emotionally wobbly.

For example, you might say something like,

> "Hey everyone, I'd like to talk about a way we can help ourselves and each other to be happier in our home and feel less emotional stress.
>
> We all know what reactive behaviour is now, right? I want us to remember that if someone at home is behaving reactively, it means they're asking for our help. It's not personal, so

we need to not take it personally. Instead, let's ask them whether they need to talk it out or just need space.

And if one of us is asked, I want us all to agree to just say what we want honestly, without feeling embarrassed or nervous about it.

Remember, the person who's asking isn't saying that we're bad or doing something wrong. They want to support us and help us figure out our own answers. They just need us to tell them what would best help us.

Can we all agree to that?"

## Let everyone know they can ask for what they need

Once you've agreed on the basics above, let everyone know that it's always – *only always* – OK for them to ask for what they need.

> It's always – *only always* – OK for them to ask for what they need.

For example, you could tell people that when YOU need space to work through something yourself, you'll ask them for it. Perhaps you could tell them that you'll probably say something like,

"Don't worry about me. I'm just doing my own stuff. I'm processing. Everything's OK.
I'll come and chat it out if I need to. Then, when I'm on the other side and am more aware of what my body's actually saying to me, I'll be happy to share it with you."

Or, if there's something you know is bothering you but you're not sure why, you might say,

"Hey, today, wow, I felt really resentful doing the washing. It's not working for me. I'm going to take a bit of space and work out what's going on. I'd appreciate it if someone else could take over. If not, no worries. I'll get to it later."

Or, if there's something you've asked for before that isn't being respected, you could say,

> "Hey, I've got this story going on, and I'd love to talk it out because I'm confused. I've continually asked for the dishes to be done after you've eaten, and I keep repeatedly asking for the same thing most days.
>
> So either your body's trying to share something, or I've got a story about receiving help that isn't supporting me. I'd love to talk about this and get your input."

Can you see how this kind of wording creates a conscious conversation, with no blaming, accusation or demands? It also easily invites in awareness for both people. That's the kind of culture you want to create in your home.

That culture starts with being clear up front that you know you'll have times when you're going to need space. When that happens, you know that it's OK for you to stop with the intention of connecting to what your emotions are saying. It doesn't mean anyone else has done anything wrong – it just means you need to figure out what's going on.

Once you've talked about how you'll ask for space, encourage the other people in your home to think about when and how they might want to ask for space too.

## Also, let everyone know it's OK to seek therapy

Another expectation to set is that it's not only acceptable but actively *encouraged* for someone to want to work with a therapist.

Creating a culture of safe, supportive, open communication is a great start for emotional healing. But sometimes we face situations that only a trained, qualified professional can help with. So everyone in your home needs to know that this is an option if they want it.

Make it clear up front that there's no shame or judgement in acknowledging a desire for professional help. In fact, let everyone know you see it as a decision to celebrate – it's clear evidence of that person wanting to heal, grow and evolve. Often, it makes things a lot easier for everyone.

> Deciding to see a therapist is clear evidence of that person wanting to heal, grow and evolve.

Tell the members of your home that if, at any point, they decide they want to work with a therapist, you'll back them 100%. And let them know that if you decide at any point it's what you want, you'd appreciate the same support from them.

## This isn't hard – it's just new

Back in Chapter 1, I let you know up front that you probably wouldn't get the techniques you learnt from this book 100% right the first time.

Remember that I compared learning these techniques to learning to ride a bicycle. I reminded you that when you first sat on a bike, you probably felt incredibly wobbly. You likely spent more time falling off than you did in the bike seat. And a few skinned knees and elbows along the way were just par for the course.

Eventually, though, you mastered the art of bike-riding – because really, with a bit of practice, it *isn't* that hard for most people.

I want to take a moment now to remind you about that bike-riding analogy because it's a great metaphor for communicating about other people's emotional stress.

Just like you weren't born knowing how to ride a bike and had to learn, the same is true of these communication techniques. You weren't born knowing how to communicate with emotional maturity. Nor were you born knowing how to value your emotions as a positive way to understand your heart's desires and who you are. And, if you're like most people, you weren't taught how to do these things as you grew up either. Instead, you probably saw adults fighting, blaming, burying, ignoring and withholding when they felt emotional stress.

So trying to learn these skills now can feel incredibly hard.

If that's the case for you, I want you to repeat these six words over and over to yourself,

> "It's not hard. It's just new."

Write them in your journal. Stick them to the bathroom mirror or the fridge. Say them out loud whenever you need to remind yourself.

I promise you that when you practise them, these techniques really do start to feel easier.

Because, really, they were never hard to start with.

They were only ever new.

## Start small and build...

The best way to get the practice you need to make these communication techniques easier is to take small steps and build on them.

You probably didn't expect to enter a 100km cross-country cycle race when you first sat on your bike as a child. First, you learnt to move the pedals with your feet so the bike actually moved forward – maybe with some training wheels attached. Then you got used to staying upright without the training wheels. Then you figured out how to cycle smoothly on the flat. Then there were hills… and so on.

Try to use the same approach with learning these communication skills. In the same way that you fell off your bike several times as you learnt to ride it, you're going to 'get it wrong' with your communication sometimes too. You're going to spin out or blow up every now and then.

So will everyone else in your house.

If this happens, once things have calmed down again, take some time to acknowledge out loud what took place. State too how you would have preferred to have shown up instead. For example, you might say,

> "Wow. I really didn't show up the way I wanted to yesterday. I'm sorry I yelled and accused you of [xxxx]. What I really wanted to communicate was [xxxx]."

Gradually, it will start taking you less and less time to calm down and recognise what happened. You may even notice yourself 'spinning out' in the moment while it's happening. If so, just tweak the words above to reflect that the yelling and accusing is happening *now*. Then express what you really want to communicate *now*.

Eventually, you'll get to the point where you're aware of the emotional stress building up and you can catch yourself before you blow up. At this point, before the spin out even happens, you'll be able to say,

> "Hey, I need to stop. I can feel emotional stress building, and I need to go away and work out why.
>
> I promise I'll come back and pick up this conversation again once I know what's going on."

Take small steps, and acknowledge and celebrate yourself every time you manage to put them into practice.

Then, if you see someone else in your home communicating with emotional maturity, acknowledge and celebrate them for it too. Nothing will create an overall emotionally happy home culture faster than recognising and reinforcing each of the small steps it takes to get there.

> *"It's your joy to discover that something that is not your joy is part of your joy."*
>
> – Bashar

## When families need to break up

Sometimes, no matter what you do, it's no longer in everyone's highest good for a family to stay together.

In my experience, 80% of the families who put these techniques into action stay together and grow far stronger than they could have dreamed of being beforehand. However, that still leaves 20% for whom separation is the best path forward.

> Walking away should never be the first course of action, but sometimes it's the best eventual outcome for everyone.

Walking away from each other should never be the first course of action. Sometimes, however, it's the best eventual outcome for everyone concerned. Nobody wants to stay in a relationship in which love has run its course. Nobody wants to stay in a relationship in which they have no love left to give. And nobody wants to stay in a relationship with someone else who has no love left to give either.

If this is where you are now, it's essential to walk away for the lightest reasons and in the lightest way. Here's what I mean.

- **First, ensure that you're taking full responsibility for your own emotional happiness.** Never walk away because 'your partner isn't making you happy'. Remember: that's not your partner's job. It never was. It's *only always* your job to make yourself happy.

    However, you might feel that you're emotionally happy with yourself and your life now, but that you'd grow and evolve far better in a different environment. If so, be willing to 'have your own back' and be honest about what you want.

- **Second, take the time and energy to end the relationship well.** Aim to move forward consciously and compassionately, creating an outcome that will provide the highest good for everyone.

    Don't blame or criticise your partner for the breakup. Rather, recognise that you're doing what you're doing *because* you believe it's the best thing for all concerned. If you have children, make sure they understand this too, rather than letting them believe that it's anybody's 'fault'.

For both of these steps, it can really help to get professional help – ideally as a couple, but individually if necessary.

You don't have to deal with it alone.

## Chapter 7 Exercise

Let's get real about the stories you carry about your childhood family members. These stories will often show up in your interactions with the people in your home in the present.

The good news is that, without invalidating anyone's past or present experiences, you can create your own story about them. And your new story can be based on what you want to see, rather than what's showing up externally.

This is a very powerful exercise – you'll just need some time, your journal and a pen to do it.

1. Choose a family member from the list below.

    - Mum
    - Step-sibling
    - Dad
    - Grandparent
    - Step-parent
    - Aunt
    - Sister
    - Uncle
    - Brother
    - Cousin

2. Write down the primary negative or limiting story you have about that family member.

    For example, you might write, "Mum never listens to me."

3. Change the story so that it reflects what you want to see from that person, and write this down.

    For example, you might write, "Mum actively listens to me and sees things from my point of view."

4. Using the belief-changing technique you learnt in Chapter 6, make this your *new* primary story whenever you think or talk about that person, or talk to them.

## Chapter 7 Summary

1. All reactive behaviours, whether in yourself or in others, are a cry for help.

2. You can *only* always choose how you'll respond to other people's reactive behaviours.

3. When someone in your home behaves reactively, it's important to offer them either space or a chance to talk things out.

4. You're not responsible for 'fixing' another person's emotional stress, and trying to do so does them a disservice.

5. Your thoughts about people matter, so choose to think about them as you want them to show up, rather than as they actually do.

6. Communication is the key to creating an emotionally happy home, and it requires feeling safe speaking from your heart, even when it's uncomfortable.

# Conclusion

## Congratulations – you're ready to start practising

Congratulations on getting to the end of this book.

If you've made it to this point, you've realised that you really can have anything your heart and higher self desire for you. No matter how deep your emotional wounds run or how long they've festered, you can heal them. And unlike a broken bone or a physical cut, once you've done the work, you'll heal back stronger and healthier than you were in the first place.

If you've made it to this point, you've *also* realised that emotional happiness isn't simply about fixing what feels broken right now. It's not just about feeling unhappy less often or repairing damaged relationships.

Yes, of course it's about those things too. But it's also about expanding and exploring, and uncovering new (or at least, hidden) gifts within yourself. It's about creating something exciting for yourself that incorporates all the good things your heart and higher self desire for you.

Finally, you've discovered that emotional happiness is also about realising you don't need to depend on anyone else (not even me) to give you your answers. The guidance and insight you've longed for are there – available and accessible within you – 24/7. All you need to do is learn how to pay attention and become aware of them.

You can grow into a genuinely better human being by using everything you've read about.

## In other words, you CAN have the life you want

To give you a final sense of the practical difference that developing spiritual intelligence and emotional maturity can make, let me introduce you to one last client, Kirsten (this is her real name)...

### Kirsten's story: complete transformation through emotional hygiene

When Kirsten first met me ten years ago, she felt like her back was against the wall. For eight years, her health had been steadily deteriorating.

It had started with a chronic fatigue diagnosis, and her weakened body had then gone on to develop other illnesses, including Ross River fever, shingles, pleurisy and glandular fever. Not surprisingly, those physical illnesses had also come with an emotional cost. Kirsten had suffered from severe depression, often having suicidal thoughts.

She'd tried working with conventional medical practitioners without any noticeable results. She read self-help book after self-help book and tried a multitude of alternative therapies. None of it had done any good, and she felt trapped and helpless.

When a friend suggested she contact me, we began to work together to uncover her emotional stress and detangle the knots of her old limiting beliefs and programs.

And, like so many of the other clients you've already met, Kirsten discovered that she had a lot going on beneath the obvious health issues. For example, she realised:

- She was addicted to work: a combination of feeling scared of not being good enough and needing to please others sometimes led to her working 24/7.
- She was deeply unhappy with her relationship: when she first got sick, she was newly married and had expected life to be a fairy tale. Instead, she found it hard to open up and ask for what she wanted, feeling ashamed that everything wasn't perfect straight away.
- She simply couldn't stop and be still: even when she wasn't working, she was trying to constantly push through whatever life threw at her. She had no idea how to connect with her heart and figure out what truly gave her joy.

Additionally, she hated that her husband kept binge-drinking and made his reactive behaviours all about her.

It took patience, time and a willingness to get uncomfortable, but eventually, Kirsten untangled each of these knots. Today, she tells everyone that she's a completely different person to that unhappy, sick woman she used to be. For example:

- She left an unfulfilling career in teaching and has now become an Emotional Stress Expert to help other families using my techniques.
- She's taken responsibility for her own emotional wellbeing and can easily talk to her husband about what she wants from their relationship.
- She can't remember the last time she was sick: it's so much easier now to listen to her body and give it the nourishment it needs, so chronic sickness has become a thing of the past.
- Best of all, she has a four-year-old son, and she feels immensely fulfilled, knowing that her growth has paved the way for his emotional health.

Perhaps you're not yet at the rock bottom stage that Kirsten was at when she first got in touch with me. If not, the good news is that you don't need to be in crisis to benefit from practising emotional hygiene and managing your emotional stress. The sooner you start working on resolving whatever emotional stress you *have* built up, the smoother and easier you'll find the process.

And, as you've learnt in this book, emotional stress management isn't just about 'fixing' the surface problems that emotional stress manifests itself as in your life. It's about going on to create the ideal life you've always wanted to live. It's about being able to tune into the guidance of your heart and higher self to first discover what that life is, and then make it happen.

Then again, maybe you *are* at the same kind of crisis point that Kirsten was. Maybe you too have tried doctor after doctor and therapy after therapy. If so, I hope her story has inspired you. Your heart and higher self drew you to these pages for a reason. Now it's time to let them guide you towards the healing and growth you long for.

> "Nobody can go back and start a new beginning, but anyone can start today and make a new ending."
>
> – Maria Robinson

## A gentle reminder: nothing will change until you do

It's one thing to learn about the tools and practices you've discovered in these pages and understand them intellectually. If you want to be emotionally happy, however, you have to do more than just understand them. You need to put them into practice.

You need to start with whatever's going on at home for you NOW – with your partner, your kids, your flatmates or your childhood family. You need to be prepared to get uncomfortable as you check in with your heart and higher self via your emotions (just like Sarah back in the Introduction) to see what's really going on.

Then, once you've gained that essential insight and awareness, you have to be prepared to act on it. EVERYTHING flows outwards from there.

Hopefully, though, you've realised that you really CAN sort this stuff out. You can see through the murky veil of your own 'stuff' enough to catch glimpses of the compassionate, loving wisdom that's hiding on the other side of it. You know – again, as we said in the Introduction – that all of this might be simple, but it's by no means easy.

And you know that even when it's hard, you can choose to be emotionally happy while you're doing it.

To get yourself to where you want to be, I hope you are making it a priority to block out time for an emotional shower every day. I believe it's *only always* the foundation of any emotional hygiene practice – and I don't think anyone can be truly emotionally healthy without some version of it.

I also hope that my words have left you ready and willing to take responsibility for your own emotional reactions.

And, finally, I hope you can at least *imagine* feeling deeply grateful (rather than defensive) when someone else lovingly tells you that you're emotionally stressed. After all, without their insight, you'd lose your chance to gain all the wisdom that's on the other side of your wobble.

If all these things are true, my work with this book is done. And I'm more grateful than I can express to have had the opportunity to share it with you.

OCEANS OF LOVE

*Jules xx*

# Need a Little More Support?

Now it is your turn to transform yourself and your home. I will support you in transforming the unknown complexity of your emotional body, directly from your heart and higher self, into a language that you can understand.

If you are ready to learn more about how this will work specifically for you and your individual circumstances, you can book a one-on-one consultation with me. The insight and awareness you will receive will transform your emotional stress into conscious clarity, leaving you feeling aligned, connected and transformed.

I also offer you the *Emotionally* HAPPY HOMES ® audio series, which is a collection of eight awesome MP3s that have been channelled directly from my higher self. Our popular membership service is also available with lots of extra tips and tools to complement what you find in the book and help you maintain an emotionally happy home.

Book your consultation or join our membership now at www.julesoneill.com and make this year your best year ever.

You can find information on the website to further your education in how to create an emotionally happy self and home.

# About the Author

For more than two decades, Jules O'Neill has helped people to create emotional harmony in themselves and their homes.

She nurtured her abilities from a young age as she sought to control her own intense emotions. Jules knew she had a gift in being able to soothe a person and help them see light in the darkest of spaces. Her next move was in learning how to understand and support her own emotional body.

Her career began on the corporate treadmill as a national buyer for a leading supermarket chain. The role gave her worldly experience, financial success and a working knowledge of corporate culture. It suited her goals for the time and the busy corporate lifestyle ticked all the boxes.

However, she felt a persistent intuitive calling to contribute more and felt drawn to the deeper appeal of bringing life to her creative dreams.

Her first business venture was a vegetarian restaurant in Parramatta, NSW. She opened 'Crank's Café' in the mid-'90s as she loved the idea of feeding people healthy, organic and fresh food. Jules also explored her interest in Neuro Emotional Technique (NET) to learn about emotional maturity. There she found solutions through exploring, unpacking and understanding what her emotions were saying, rather than avoiding or suppressing them.

Jules and her partner then worked on creating their emotional self-healing system called Neuro Stress Release (NSR). Following that was the creation of Women's Wisdom®, a tailored program helping women become emotionally self-aware in their families and homes.

Seeing the profound results of these programs ignited her passion to help individuals facing severe and confronting challenges. She went on to develop a modality called Body Consciousness®. This comprehensive program enabled her to transform some of the biggest, tightest internal knots that people suffered from due to emotional stress. These unconscious conditionings could then be healed, transformed and managed.

Jules understood from her professional observations that phenomenal transformation occurred when people addressed the emotional stress in their own homes. After 20 years of helping tens of thousands of people with their life issues and emotional conundrums, she has intuited the *Emotionally* HAPPY HOMES ® healing system and concepts.

These lifelong insights come together in the book Jules shares with you now. She knows it will empower you to naturally live a healthy, fulfilling, peaceful, creative life and transform your home into a place of love, connection, warmth and creativity.

APPENDIX A

# Negative Emotions

*"Like the day finds its morning light,
you will find your way again."*

– Dhiman

## List of emotions

You can find some possible definitions of each emotion on the pages that follow this one.

- Afraid
- Angry
- Anxious
- Ashamed
- Avoidant
- Bitter
- Blamed
- Bored
- Broken-hearted
- Burdened
- Confused
- Criticised
- Devastated
- Disconnected
- Dominated
- Doubtful
- Downtrodden
- Drained
- Dramatic
- Empty

- Explosive
- Failing
- Fragile
- Frustrated
- Grief-struck
- Guilty
- Heavy
- Held back
- Humiliated
- Irritated
- Impatient
- Jealous
- Lifeless
- Lonely
- Lost
- Misunderstood
- Nothing
- Obligated
- Overwhelmed
- Paranoid

- Passive
- Pressured
- Regretful
- Rejected
- Resentful
- Self-pitying
- Sick
- Suspicious
- Stuck
- Trapped
- Uncomfortable
- Undermined
- Unloved
- Unsafe
- Unsettled
- Victimised
- Vulnerable
- Weak
- Worn out

# Definitions of each emotion

*Note: I've collected these definitions from a multitude of sources over time and reworded them to make them my own.*

## Afraid
1. Feeling the all-consuming emotion of terror, fright or panic
2. In extreme distress, anxiety and doubt
3. Scared or having a phobic response

## Angry
1. Feeling very annoyed, often about an insult or a wrong
2. Expressing extreme annoyance
3. Stormy-looking

## Anxious
1. Uneasy, concerned or distressed
2. Worried about future outcomes
3. Tending to negatively prejudge future events
4. In a morbid state of excessive or unrealistic uneasiness or dread

## Ashamed
1. Humiliated, embarrassed, discomfited or disgraced
2. Feeling as though you've brought dishonour, scandal, contempt or disrepute upon yourself or others
3. Regretful, remorseful, guilty or as though you've lost face

## Avoidant
1. Wanting to sidestep, dodge or evade a situation or person
2. Wanting to cop out
3. Wanting to consciously hide from, elude or ignore something or someone

### Bitter
1. Resentful, begrudging or discontented
2. Spiteful, sour, unpleasant or vindictive
3. Nasty, cruel, upsetting or hostile
4. Venomous, vicious, savage or antagonistic

### Blamed
1. Feeling as though someone considers you responsible for something wrong or unfortunate that has happened
2. Feeling as though someone is criticising, accusing or finding fault with you
3. Feeling as though someone considers you guilty of an inappropriate act

### Bored
1. Tired of and slightly annoyed by a person or situation that is not interesting, exciting or entertaining
2. Having or showing no interest in somebody or something
3. Having reached the limits of tolerance or patience with somebody or something

### Broken-hearted
1. Extremely sad
2. Intensely unhappy or disappointed because of something that has happened
3. Feeling as though a promise has been broken, or not honoured or fulfilled
4. Destroyed or badly hurt by grief or misfortune
5. Split apart, eg. by divorce, separation or desertion

### Burdened
1. Heavy with a responsibility, duty, obligation or task
2. Overwhelmed, taxed, under strain or harassed
3. Feeling as though you're carrying a load

Confused
1. Unable to think intelligently
2. Unable to make a logical or sensible order out of matters
3. Embarrassed and not knowing what to say or how to act
4. Disoriented

Criticised
1. Feeling as though you're under some form of verbal attack, disapproval, abuse or chastisement
2. Feeling as though someone has expressed disapproval of you

Devastated
1. Feeling as though someone or something has ruined you
2. Feeling as though someone or something has destroyed you
3. Feeling overwhelmed

Disconnected
1. Separate from someone or something
2. Feeling no connection or relationship to someone or something

Dominated
1. Feeling as though someone or something has control, power or authority over you
2. Feeling as though someone is towering above you

Doubtful
1. Uncertain, hesitant, confused or suspicious
2. Feeling that something is unlikely, is dubious or lacks conviction
3. Apprehensive, uneasy or having reservations about something
4. Tentative, ambivalent, divided or in two minds

Downtrodden
1. Having only so much left
2. Unhappy and gloomy
3. Down-at-the-heels, shabby and neglected

Drained
1. Empty of physical, mental or emotional energy
2. Exhausted, depleted and consumed by something

Dramatic
1. Large in degree or scale, and often occurring with surprising suddenness

Empty
1. Purposeless, worthless, valueless or hollow
2. Unfulfilled, aimless or of no use
3. Feeling a sense that life is futile, meaningless, unsatisfactory or insignificant

Explosive
1. Likely to explode
2. Likely to express violent anger
3. Sudden and dramatic

Failing
1. Feeling a sense of defeat, lack of success, collapse or disappointment
2. Feeling incompetent, or like a loser, non-achiever or 'no hoper'
3. Feeling as though you haven't come through with the goods, have let someone down, haven't come up to scratch or have no confidence

Fragile
1. Easily broken, flimsy or brittle
2. Of a delicate disposition – vulnerable, failing or weak
3. Easily threatened or destroyed, or unsound

### Frustrated
1. Annoyed, angry, irritated, bitter and resentful
2. Feeling a sense of failure due to being blocked, thwarted or hindered

### Grief-struck
1. Sorrowing, sad or despairing
2. The resulting emotion from a broken heart, torment, anguish or emotional pain
3. Feeling bitter, regret or remorse, hardship and suffering

### Guilty
1. Ashamed, disgraced, repentant or remorseful
2. Having a guilty conscience
3. Wearing the heaviness, blame and sin of misconduct

### Heavy
1. Feeling weighed down
2. Needing much strength and effort
3. Demanding
4. Affected by tiredness
5. Serious and oppressive

### Held back
1. Feeling as though something or someone is in your way
2. Feeling as though something is a burden on you

### Humiliated
1. Feeling as though someone has damaged your dignity or pride, especially publicly
2. Embarrassed, ashamed or having lost face
3. Ridiculed, picked on or joked about

Irritated
1. Annoyed by somebody or something
2. Stimulated in a way that provokes a response

Impatient
1. Annoyed at waiting
2. Eager to do something immediately, and unwilling to wait
3. Easily annoyed

Jealous
1. Bitter and unhappy because of another's advantages, possessions or luck
2. Suspicious about a rival's or competitor's influence, especially in regard to a loved one
3. Possessively watchful of something
4. Demanding exclusive loyalty or adherence

Lifeless
1. Lacking excitement or animation
2. Dead, or seeming to be dead

Lonely
1. Sad through being without friends or company
2. Isolated and rarely visited
3. Without companionship or support from other people

Lost
1. Misplaced, off-course, off the right track, disoriented and confused in the present situation
2. Hopeless, despairing, adrift or astray in your life direction
3. Engrossed, absorbed, immersed or preoccupied in your own thoughts or world

Misunderstood
1. Not correctly understood
2. Not properly and sympathetically appreciated

Nothing
1. Not feeling a single thing
2. Feeling as though you're not a single part of anything
3. Feeling as though you have no quality
4. Feeling as though you don't exist

Obligated
1. Bound, committed or forced
2. Pressured, burdened or concerned
3. Feeling as though you're in someone's debt, or feeling liable for something

Overwhelmed
1. Emotionally affected in a complete or irresistible way
2. Feeling as though someone has used superior strength, force or numbers to defeat you completely
3. Feeling as though something has flowed over you and submerged or covered you completely

Paranoid
1. Obsessively anxious about something
2. Unreasonably suspicious of other people and their thoughts or motives

Passive
1. Tending not to participate actively, and usually letting others make decisions
2. Tending to submit or obey without arguing or resisting
3. Influenced by something external

Pressured
1. The feeling of being under stress, strain or force
2. Feeling coerced, influenced, brainwashed or intimidated
3. Feeling as though someone is twisting your arm

Regretful
1. Sorry for something

Rejected
1. Feeling as though someone hasn't accepted you
2. Feeling as though someone has turned you down
3. Feeling as though someone has been unkind to you

Resentful
1. Annoyed about having been badly treated, or characterised by such a feeling of annoyance

Self-pitying
1. Pitying yourself, especially exaggerated or self-indulgent pity, concerning your own difficulties and hardships

Sick
1. Deeply affected by some unpleasant feeling, eg. sorrow, disgust or boredom

Suspicious
1. Doubtful, unsure, distrustful or disbelieving
2. A tendency to see circumstances as questionable, odd, strange or dubious

Stuck
1. Jammed, caught or held in an immovable position
2. Not able to find a solution or way out of a situation

Trapped
1. Caged or confined
2. Ambushed, tricked or taken unaware, such that the person trapping you puts you at a disadvantage or in their power

Uncomfortable
1. Not physically comfortable
2. Awkward and ill at ease

Undermined
1. Diminished or gradually weakened by something
2. Feeling as though someone has weakened, discredited or destroyed you by covert and malicious action

Unloved
1. Without love and acceptance from others or yourself
2. Without feelings of being nurtured or cared for by others or yourself
3. Without feelings of tender affection from somebody or yourself

Unsafe
1. Likely to experience harm or injury

Unsettled
1. Not decided or uncertain
2. Changeable
3. Lacking order or stability

Victimised
1. Suffering from a destructive or injurious action
2. Feeling deceived or cheated, either by your own emotions, ignorance of the dishonesty of others, or by some impersonal agency

Vulnerable
1. Without adequate protection
2. Easily persuadable or liable to give in to temptation
3. Unable to resist illness, debility or failure
4. Open to attack

Weak
1. Not mentally strong or physically fit
2. Easily overcome or defeated
3. Not having strength of character
4. Not powerful or intense
5. Not having particular skills or abilities

Worn Out
1. So damaged or affected as to no longer be able to operate
2. Very tired
3. No longer relevant, useful or fashionable

APPENDIX B

# Positive Emotions

*"The best day of your life is the one on which you decide your life is your own."*

– Bob Moawad

## List of emotions

You can find some possible definitions of each emotion on the pages that follow this one.

- Accepted
- Adventurous
- Amazed
- Ambitious
- Approved of
- Aroused
- Assertive
- Authentic
- Clear
- Committed
- Composed
- Confident
- Creative
- Curious
- Detached
- Determined
- Empowered
- Energised
- Enough
- Free
- Flexible
- Grateful
- Friendly
- Happy
- Included
- Independent
- Joyful
- Light
- Loving
- Natural
- Noticed
- Nurtured
- Open
- Optimistic
- Organised
- Passionate
- Patient
- Playful
- Profound
- Proud
- Ready
- Realised
- Relieved
- Safe
- Satisfied
- Saved
- Sensual
- Sexual
- Skilled
- Solid
- Stable
- Supported
- Tender
- Trusting
- Valued
- Vulnerable
- Warm

## Definitions of each emotion

*Note: again, I've collected these definitions from a multitude of sources over time and reworded them to make them my own.*

### Accepted
1. Feeling a sense of being received
2. Welcomed, embraced, approved of or adopted into a group

### Adventurous
1. Daring, intrepid, bold or venturesome
2. Fearless, brave, undaunted or confident

### Amazed
1. Having a sense of something being so extraordinary or wonderful as to be barely believable or to cause extreme surprise
2. Seeing something as outstanding

### Ambitious
1. Having a strong desire for success
2. Strongly desirous

### Approved of
1. Accepted, agreed with, consented to or blessed
2. Validated, confirmed, supported or backed
3. Admired, respected or encouraged

### Aroused
1. To have a feeling, response or desire evoked
2. To have sexual desire stimulated

### Assertive
1. Confident in feeling or action
2. Forcefully strong and noticeable

Authentic
1. Genuine and original, as opposed to being fake or a reproduction
2. Trustworthy
3. Valid
4. Genuine

Clear
1. Comprehensible, straightforward and direct
2. Transparent
3. Free of, relieved and no longer affected by

Committed
1. Devoted to somebody or something such as a cause or relationship
2. Wholeheartedly devoted to a goal, cause or job

Composed
1. Not agitated or distracted
2. Without anxiety or strong emotion
3. Feeling that you're holding it together

Confident
1. Self-assured, positive and assertive without ego
2. Optimistic, hopeful and sure in your belief
3. Firmly trusting and expectant

Creative
1. Able to create things
2. Using imagination to create new ideas or things
3. Making imaginative use of the limited resources available

Curious
1. Eager to know something
2. Inquisitive

Detached
1. Not attached to something
2. Separate from something
3. Free from emotional involvement
4. Able to walk away or leave behind

Determined
1. Resolute, purposeful and firm in one's mind
2. Adamant, decided, persistent and relentless in striving to achieve a goal
3. Obsessive about, hell-bent or totally committed to

Empowered
1. Given authority by somebody
2. Confident or assertive

Energised
1. Enlivened, invigorated and motivated
2. Having power supplied to get going and active
3. Dynamic, excited and 'pepped up'

Enough
1. Feeling as though you have as much as you need
2. Feeling as though you are all you need to be in all areas

Free
1. Able to act freely
2. Feeling as though you've been released from captivity or slavery
3. Able to speak freely

Flexible
1. Able to bend without breaking
2. Able to adapt to new situations

3. Supple, mouldable, pliable and adaptable – mentally, physically and emotionally
4. Willing to compromise, cooperate or tolerate

Grateful
1. Feeling gratitude or being thankful
2. Feeling gratified that someone or something has given you pleasure or done you a favour
3. Appreciative of, and inclined to return, a kindness

Friendly
1. Warm and compassionate to another person
2. Congenial, good-natured and kindly
3. Affectionate and easygoing

Happy
1. Delighted, pleased or glad
2. Characterised by or indicative of pleasure, contentment or joy
3. Cheerful or willing

Included
1. Contained within a group
2. Feeling like a part of a group

Independent
1. Not controlled by another person
2. Able to function by yourself
3. Self-supporting
4. Confident in yourself

Joyful
1. Feeling, bringing, causing or showing joy
2. Feeling or showing pleasure or contentment
3. Causing pleasure

### Light
1. Happy-go-lucky
2. Cheerfully optimistic and hopeful
3. Easygoing
4. Jovial, in good spirits, welcoming
5. Comfortable in yourself, regardless of circumstances

### Loving
1. Deeply affectionate, fond and tender
2. Devoted, adoring or passionate
3. Enjoying, relishing or taking delight in

### Natural
1. Innate, rather than acquired
2. Representing something in a way that seems true to life
3. Patient with the unfolding of things
4. A knowing that things will come to you easily

### Noticed
1. Having attention paid
2. Observed
3. Recognised
4. Acknowledged

### Nurtured
1. Feeling taken care of
2. Feeling encouraged to flourish
3. Supported to shine

### Open
1. Having no problem or concealing cover
2. Completely obvious or blatant
3. Free from limitations, boundaries or restrictions

4. Willing to consider or deal with something
5. Not yet decided, or subject to further thought

## Optimistic
1. Having a positive attitude
2. Hopeful

## Organised
1. Feeling as though you're working in a systematic and efficient way

## Passionate
1. Feeling sexual desire
2. Intensely emotional
3. Enthusiastic
4. Having strong emotions

## Patient
1. Tolerant, restrained, composed and understanding
2. Persevering, persistent, enduring and purposeful
3. Calm, tranquil, serene and considerate in character

## Playful
1. Feeling of enjoying fun and games
2. Feeling of saying or doing something in fun
3. Light and easy
4. Childlike

## Profound
1. Coming from deep inside
2. Coming from the depths of your being
3. Able to penetrate beyond what is superficial or obvious

### Proud
1. Pleased, happy or delighted with
2. Satisfied, fulfilled, rewarded, gratified or appreciative
3. Self-respecting, dignified, noble and independent
4. Magnificent, grand, majestic or distinguished

### Ready
1. Prepared, usually in advance, for something
2. Willing to do something

### Realised
1. Feeling that you know and understand something
2. Aware of something
3. Feeling that you've achieved something

### Relieved
1. Feeling that something unpleasant has stopped
2. Feeling that your burden has eased
3. Feeling that someone has helped you by removing something

### Safe
1. Not dangerous
2. Unharmed or undamaged
3. Sure to be successful
4. Cautious and conservative

### Satisfied
1. Happy, contented and pleased with yourself
2. Fulfilled, gratified and appeased
3. Convinced, certain, sure or easy in your own mind

Saved
1. Feeling rescued by somebody or something
2. Feeling spared by somebody or something from something else
3. Feeling prevented from doing something (usually something that would be harmful) by someone else

Sensual
1. Relating to the body or the senses as opposed to the mind or the intellect
2. Relating to physical, or especially sexual, pleasure

Sexual
1. Feeling something relating to sex, sexuality or the sexual organs
2. Feeling something that relates to the two sexes

Skilled
1. Able to do something well
2. Able to do something that requires training well

Solid
1. Not soft or yielding
2. Able to be relied or depended upon

Stable
1. Not changing
2. Not likely to move
3. Not excitable

Supported
1. Stable
2. Able to bear weight
3. Being sustained financially by someone
4. Being given active help and encouragement

5. Having someone who's present and giving encouragement
6. Having someone who's giving assistance or comfort
7. Having someone who enables you to live

Tender
1. Careful and gentle in feeling
2. Sensitive and caring towards others, and often feeling emotions intensely

Trusting
1. Tending to have belief, faith or confidence in others or yourself
2. Free from suspicion or doubt
3. Able to rely on someone

Valued
1. Given monetary worth
2. Given full worth
3. Given importance
4. Given meaning

Vulnerable
1. Willing to show up and be seen in all your human imperfection
2. Willing to have an uncomfortable conversation
3. Willing to take action despite having no idea of the outcome

Warm
1. Kind and friendly
2. Passionate or lively
3. Greatly enthusiastic

## APPENDIX C

# Reactive Behaviours

*"You will be put again and again into nearly impossible situations. They will attempt again and again through subterfuge, guise and force to make you submit, quit and/or die quietly inside."*

– Charles Bukowski

## List of behaviours

- (Developing or having an) Addiction
- Attention-seeking
- Blaming
- Boasting
- (Being) Bossy
- (Being) Cautious
- (Acting) Co-dependently
- (Being) Competitive
- Complaining
- Controlling
- Covering up
- Criticising
- (Being) Defensive
- Denying
- (Being) Disorganised
- Dumping
- Exaggerating
- (Going to) Extremes
- (Acting from) Fear
- Fidgeting
- Giving up
- (Being) Greedy
- (Being) Harsh
- Hiding
- Ignoring
- (Being) Impatient
- (Acting) Insanely
- (Acting) Insecurely
- (Being) Lazy
- (Having) Low self-esteem
- (Being) Loud
- Manipulating
- (Being) Never satisfied
- Over-pleasing
- (Acting from) Perfectionism
- (Acting from) Pessimism
- (Being) Phobic
- (Being) Picky
- (Being) Possessive
- Projecting
- Procrastinating
- Quitting
- (Being) Rash
- Rescuing
- (Being) Rude
- Rushing
- (Speaking with) Sarcasm
- Self-pitying
- (Being) Selfish
- (Being) Sceptical
- Teasing
- (Being) Unapproachable
- (Being) Uncommunicative
- (Being) Unconscious
- (Being) Vague
- (Being) Wasteful

www.ingramcontent.com/pod-product-compliance
Lightning Source LLC
Chambersburg PA
CBHW070547010526
44118CB00012B/1252